D1348474

DUBLIN

In the Age of William Butler Yeats and James Joyce

DUBLIN

In the Age of William Butler Yeats
and James Joyce

By Richard M. Kain

DAVID & CHARLES: NEWTON ABBOT

Books by Richard M. Kain

Fabulous Voyager: James Joyce's Ulysses
With Marvin Magalaner, *Joyce: The Man, the Work, the Reputation*
Dublin in the Age of William Butler Yeats and James Joyce

ISBN 0 7153 5425 6

© The University of Oklahoma Press,
Publishing Division of the University 1962

First published in Great Britain 1972

Reproduced and Printed in Great Britain by
Redwood Press Limited, Trowbridge & London
for David & Charles (Publishers) Limited
Newton Abbot   Devon

For My Irish Friends

Preface

DUBLIN has long been celebrated as a birthplace of poets and patriots. It has been admired for the classical elegance, albeit faded, of its public edifices and residential squares. Above all, it is cherished for a way of life, humane and raffish, trivial and profound, which it has maintained since the days of the debonair Earl of Chesterfield. The late Oliver St. John Gogarty, so characteristic a product of Dublin, once exclaimed: "How I love the old town, where every man is a potential idler, poet or friend."

This volume describes some aspects of Dublin in its recent period of glory when it was the scene of a literary revival and the setting for a war of independence. So extensively has this period been documented that acknowledgments of printed sources should be almost innumerable. I wish to express my personal gratitude to those who, for me, have exemplified something of the Irish spirit. It is a privilege to record my memories of Mrs. James Joyce, of Mr. Gogarty, ever-refreshing font of wisdom and humor, and of two notable bibliophiles, the perceptive editor of the *Dublin Magazine* Seumas O'Sullivan, and the patriot-historian P. S. O'Hegarty. To their names I am happy to add those of Constantine Curran, Mrs. William Butler Yeats, former President Sean T. O'Kelly, President Eamon de Valera, Austin Clarke, Sean O'Faolain, Michael Scott, and Niall Sheridan.

To my colleagues at the University of Louisville, to many unnamed students of things Irish, to helpful book dealers, to librarians, particularly those of the National Library of Ireland, and to my Irish friends I wish to extend thanks. For their careful reading of parts of the manuscript and their valuable suggestions, I am especially grateful to Denis Donoghue of the University College, Dublin; to Oliver Edwards of the University College, Derry; and to Patrick Henchy and Thomas O'Neill of the National Library of Ireland. Mr. Alan Denson graciously gave me access to the manuscript of his scholarly edition of Æ's letters, since published. The co-operation of the University of Oklahoma Press, and the enthusiasm and insight of its editors, have made this book possible. My lasting personal debt is to my family, not only for their forbearance, which has always been great, but also for their incisive and constructive comments on the text.

R. M. K.

Louisville, Kentucky

Contents

DUBLIN

In the Age of William Butler Yeats and James Joyce

I - The Cultural Renaissance

THE romantic glow of the Irish revival still pervades Dublin. Despite the political and social revolutions which separate modern Ireland from the time of William Butler Yeats (1865–1939) and James Joyce (1882–1941), a steady flow of evaluations and reminiscences testifies to Dublin's memory, not only of the masters but also of the galaxy of notable people who surrounded them. Dublin, which questions so many things, no longer doubts the eminence of Yeats and Joyce, although it may smile at the annual influx of eager scholars from America with copies of *Ulysses* in their hands. Such visitors may be excused for thinking that their idols stood alone on the cultural horizon. The writers themselves were responsible, for, with the egotism of genius, they placed themselves in the foreground and created the impression that their city was a cultural desert.

Today the Gaelic League and the Irish Volunteers are as vivid to Dubliners as is the early Abbey Theatre. In fact, Ireland's political and artistic resurgences coincided.

After one hundred years of provincial obscurity Dublin was becoming a lively center as the new century got under way. No other literary movement of the time was attracting so much attention as the Irish renaissance. The theater was bringing to the stage a poetic quality long absent from commercial entertainments of New York's Broadway or London's West End. The first American literary visitors began to arrive, the New York patron and collector John Quinn, and the professor from the University of Pennsylvania, Cornelius Weygandt, both coming to Dublin in the summer of 1902. A year later news of the literary revival was given to audiences from Canada to California by William Butler Yeats on his first American speaking tour.

At the same time, Ireland was being reborn as a nation. A sense of mission filled the air. In this period of noble beginnings, the past was rediscovered and the future charted. Plans, literary manifestoes, and political programs aired competing claims of patriotism and culture. In the debates on the creation of a national consciousness, controversy lent zest to the argument. An astonishing number of remarkable men and women emergèd. Few countries, regardless of size, have enjoyed such a flowering as that of Ireland during the fifty years of Yeats's career, from 1889 to 1939. There were Wilde and Shaw (away in London), and Synge as well as Joyce and Yeats, and the most interesting theatre of the time, and enough novelists, poets, and painters to do credit to any nation. Yet Ireland was and is small, its population comparable to that of Iowa or Kentucky in the United States. The country lacks natural resources. It has also suffered from centuries of exploitation. Hence, little more than bare survival might be expected.

The Irish have captured the world's imagination, and the game of interpreting them has been going on for centuries, often with doubtful results. It seems impossible to distill the essence of the Irish spirit, to analyze its blend of practical and poetic, humorous and fantastic, sentimental and cynical. In a contest for the best selection of books on Ireland, a reader of the Irish periodical *The Bell* in 1946 threw in the sponge, exclaiming, "Not all the books in Trinity College Library, the National Library, the Royal Dublin Society, or the three-penny-a-week libraries would help anyone, foreign or native, to understand this isle." Sean O'Faolain's story *Persecution Mania* depicts Ike Dignam as the victim of trying to act Irish. But he could never be sure just what that was:

> He has a notion that the Irish have a gift for fantasy, so he is constantly talking fey. He also has a notion that the Irish have a magnificent gift for malice, mixed up with another idea of the Irish as great realists, so that he loves to abuse everybody for not having more common sense. But as he also believes that the Irish are the most kind and charitable people in the world he ends up every tirade with an "Ah, sure, God help us, maybe the poor fellow is good at heart."

Irish versatility is exemplified in the activities of George William Russell, one of the acknowledged leaders of the Irish revival. After cycling from town to town inspecting dairies, he might return to Dublin to supervise the publication of a journal, conduct a meeting of a theosophical society, or act the host to guests spellbound by his conversation. Russell led two lives, or more, under two names, using his own name in his work as publicist and man of affairs and adopting the occult pseudonym "Æ" (from "æon") in his role as poet and painter of the spirit world.

It is hardly an accident, then, that Irish writers, from Jonathan Swift and Richard Brinsley Sheridan to Oscar Wilde and George Bernard Shaw, have reveled in paradox. The confrontation of two opposing cultures has much to do with it. The Irishman's vivacious imagination is always titillated by Saxon stolidity. To the Irish, the English are the funniest when they are the most serious, and English common sense often seems to them the most outrageously uncommon nonsense. It almost appears that, since no one understands the Irish—not even the Irish themselves—the best thing to say about these charming people is the opposite of whatever has just been said. G. K. Chesterton once called them "the men that God made mad." The celebrated wit Sir John Mahaffy remarked that "In Ireland the inevitable never happens, the unexpected always."

The result is that anyone who writes about Ireland had better keep tongue in cheek, even at the risk of having it bitten off. The fate of his predecessors is not encouraging. In 1806, for instance, an English traveler, John Carr, published *The Stranger in Ireland,* a fair enough sort of book to the average reader. The mixture of pedestrian description, prosaic detail, and tedious narrative has served to fill many books before and since Carr's time. But the favorite prey for Irish wit is the bore. It takes the scalpel of a Swift or a Joyce to probe mediocrity with the meticulous and merciless art of parody.

Carr had written successful books on France and the Baltic, but now his subject was Ireland. Within a year an amusing satire appeared, in the form of directions for writing a book like Carr's. The gibes are delicious. An author is advised to proceed in just the same way as the Englishman had. One must praise other writers and refer to one's own books. It will make friends and help sales. One must attempt joviality, tell jokes even though they are not very funny, use plenty of platitudes, write elegantly, and be sure to omit nothing tedious or silly. Above all, learn the art of padding. Copy generously, list everything you can—"It will make many quarto pages."

Mr. Carr, now Sir John, was very unhappy, and doubly so when his suit against the publishers of *My Pocket Book* was lost in court. Even less fortunate was one Richard Twiss. Ireland was bewildering to him, for there he experienced what he called "intellectual retrogression"; that is, the more he heard the less he understood! He received a strange commemoration, his picture being used to decorate chamber pots manufactured in Dublin. An indecent epigram on the theme was forthwith written by Lady Clare, the Lord Chancellor's wife.

Of all who have commented on the Irish temperament, Oscar Wilde probably came closest to the truth. When he arrived in New York for a lecture tour, the young dandy flaunted his velvet jacket and flowing tie, announcing to an astonished customs official, "I have nothing to declare but my genius." Genius the Irish have certainly had in abundance. Their imaginative energy seems inexhaustible. It finds expression in their love for poetry and legend, in their cultivation of eccentricity and their delight in personality. Above all, it is apparent in their gift of phrase.

Despite their protests against being caricatured as "stage Irishmen," no people have been so ready to take the stage. Witness George Bernard Shaw, who missed few opportunities of holding the limelight. A delight to cartoonists and reporters, his satanic red beard and gaunt figure known to

7

millions, Shaw played the role of Puck to three generations. His technique was Irish too. He, who learned so
much from Oscar Wilde, once explained that "My method
is to take the utmost trouble to find the right thing to say
and then to say it with the utmost levity."

In Dublin, conversation is still considered an art, and
society has long been a career open to verbal talents. The
eighteenth-century *bon vivant* Sir Jonah Barrington extolled "that glow of well-bred, witty, and cordial vinous
conviviality" which he found unique in the Irish capital.
Without benefit of spirits, the teetotaler Shaw had much
the same animation. Barrington, not much of a statesman,
regarded his seat in the Irish Parliament primarily as a
social cachet, an opportunity to associate with "legislators
whose good-breeding, wit, and conviviality were mingled
with political and general information." He ranked his
friends by their wit, which is perhaps better than judging
them by money or position. One was fine in anecdote, another in repartee, another in mimicry. And there were the
outrageous bulls of Sir Boyle Roche, "the most celebrated
and entertaining anti-grammarian in the Irish Parliament." Sir Boyle and his hearers alike recognized the
pertinence of his impertinence. His most famous bull was
no more illogical than Ireland's position under English
rule. In commenting on the nation's imminent loss of its
Parliament (abolished by an Act of Union in 1800), he
exclaimed: "It would surely be better, Mr. Speaker, to give
up not only a part, but, if necessary, even the whole, of
our constitution, to preserve the remainder!"

Those who love Dublin feel that it retains an atmosphere which has all but disappeared elsewhere. One is
reminded of the clubbable London where Dr. Johnson

loved "to sit and have his talk out." Even then Dublin claimed superiority, according to an English visitor who described *Hibernia Curiosa* in 1769, and made the grudging admission that "there is a native sprightliness and sociability, a spirit of generosity and frankness in their general manner, that is conspicuous and engaging, and that cannot fail to recommend them to strangers."

Dublin speech is proverbial for grammatical purity, melody, and content. The same visitor considered this a "vain presumption," but one so widespread "that an Englishman can hardly pass a day in Dublin . . . without finding this the topic of conversation somewhere." The claim is constantly repeated. Stephen Dedalus, the fictional mask of Joyce, supplied the word "tundish" to the college dean, adding with a smile that the word comes from the suburb of Lower Drumcondra, "where they speak the best English." The New York *Times* column "Speaking of Books" reported current Irish opinion on July 16, 1950. Several writers admitted Irish eminence, recalling earlier Irish masters—Swift, Goldsmith, Burke, Shaw, and Joyce. Shaw himself called the notion nonsensical, as did Sean O'Casey, Sean O'Faolain, and Lennox Robinson. The latter, however, did make the observation that poetry is still discussed in Dublin pubs, and O'Faolain argued that Irish usage remained "free rich witty fluxive [sic]" because of its Gaelic roots and the seventeenth-century tradition.

The soft Dublin accent conveys warmth, and lilting modulations express nuances of sentiment, gaiety, and sly malice. The visitor is constantly delighted at the turns of speech which come so easily to Irish tongues. Metaphor is living and unaffected. John, the father of William Butler Yeats, remarked that by marrying the poet's mother, Susan

Pollexfen, of a substantial merchant and shipowner family, "I have given a tongue to the sea cliffs." In the shy countenance of his brother-in-law George, "his eyes seemed to peep at you like stars in the early twilight." A niece of Lady Gregory's recalled her childhood as she showed the present writer the famous autographed beech tree at Coole: "We ran up and down the garden like hares." An office boy described one of James Joyce's sisters: "She's a Joyce all right; she has the same forget-me-not blue eyes and the same penwiper nose." Politicians are especially vulnerable to shafts of Dublin wit. The success of one was attributed to the fact that "he was neither the first nor the last to run from the British." Nor are localities exempt: "He says proudly, 'I come from Cork,' and why wouldn't anyone be glad to come *from* there?" Dublin conversation can be as intoxicating as the hospitality. Charles Duff, in his delightful book on *Ireland and the Irish* (1953), tells how his English friend, safely aboard the Holyhead boat, confessed: "My head is still reeling with all that talk, isn't yours?" Harold Laski had never heard more brilliant conversation—or more nonsense—in one hour than he had in Dublin.

There are reasons for the brilliance and perhaps for the nonsense too. Yeats used to recall Oscar Wilde's remark that "we are the greatest talkers since the Greeks." Each of the major figures in the revival was reputed a master conversationalist. Among them the elder Yeats apparently had been a delightful talker and one to appreciate good speech. He noted the frequent use of poetic metaphor among the Irish, quoting a servant's welcome to a returning priest: "While you were away, there was a colour of loneliness in the air." He expressed the national disdain for material success in his definition of a gentleman as "a man not wholly occupied in getting on." His candor saved him from sentimentality. Destined first for the ministry, and then for the law, he became a skeptic who stood in the doorway during church services in order to glimpse the glories of the Irish sea and sky.

One of his son's favorite quotations was the succinct rejoinder of the Anglo-Irish philosopher Bishop George Berkeley, "We Irishmen think otherwise." The trait is widespread, along with humor and imagination, a delight in diversity, the sense of life as a play in which one can be both actor and audience, and a feeling for the pathos and the mystery of existence.

The eighteenth-century aristocracy of wealth had been followed by an aristocracy of intelligence, but neither had been able to cope with poverty, that Achilles' heel of most societies. Famine and emigration, restrictive leglislation and the consequent lack of industrial development, and the absence of raw materials took their toll. The slums of Dublin were notoriously the worst in western Europe. Their shabbiness was all the more marked because the tenement districts included once-fashionable north-side squares and Georgian terraces. Handsome mansions of the classical age were abandoned to decay. Beautifully proportioned drawing rooms, with marble mantels and stuccoed ceilings, swarmed with ragged mothers and squalling children. Buildings designed for one privileged family housed as many as fifty to one hundred people. Row after row of stately façades, now marred with broken windows, peeling paint, and trash in entries, became breeding places for disease and desperation. The death rate (forty-six per thousand) was almost three times that of English cities at the time. From such an inferno of squalor escape might seem impossible, yet it fostered Sean O'Casey, and from it arose the lyric gaiety of his tragic comedies. Joyce's background was only slightly better, his improvident father always doing his best to ruin the family, which clung perilously to respectability.

In an age of mass amusements, mass communications, and mass employment, Irish individuality is doubly welcome. There is more companionship in a Dublin pub than in any "togetherness" that Madison Avenue has dreamed of. Refugees from central overheating are sure to respond to the uncertain warmth of a peat fire. Interest in personality gives rise to a characteristic tolerance and humor, so that even the most sentimental of songs about Irish charm and Irish eyes have a good deal of truth. But a sense of fatalism gives an edge to conversation which keeps it from maudlin sentimentality. Lynn Doyle quotes a good-humored townsman in the West Country: "I think," he said, referring to the recent Civil War, "this must be the last country God made.—But then wasn't He very good to make it at all?" Ireland never "progressed" as far as industrialism, and consequently the country preserves some of the amenities which have elsewhere been destroyed.

Dublin is a city of memories: reminders of the past are never far distant. Even if broken windowpanes are common on Georgian façades, and noble fanlights often display religious images or commercial signs, doorways and stairs recall the eighteenth century, when the town was a center of fashion, rivaling London in taste and elegance. The foreground has certainly changed, with queues at every movie palace, and push carts of cheap missionary papers at corners. Until midnight unwashed urchins dodge about railings in O'Connell Street, playing tag, begging for pennies. If such Dickensian scenes might appall proud Protestants of the Enlightenment, there is nevertheless a bustle of life on Dublin streets. Some of the worst slums have been razed, but the tower of St. Patrick's Cathedral still evokes the figure of Dean Swift, proud and angry in defiance of unjust authority. The tenacity of tradition is seen in the fact that when the ravages of revolution destroyed three landmarks of classic Dublin—the Four Courts, the Customs House, and the General Post Office—attempts to replace them in some pseudo "Hibernian Romanesque" style were resisted, and the fine structures were carefully restored according to plans and sketches of the original buildings.

Most cities could well envy the setting. The blue haze on near-by hills seems to cloak the dwelling place of ancient heroes. Not far off is the ford where the Irish Siegfried, Cuchulain, withstood the enemy host. In the soft mist one can imagine the sighs of the brokenhearted captive, Deirdre of the Sorrows. Gulls perched on trawlers in the Liffey remind us of the proximity of the Irish Sea, over which Tristan ventured. Tradition has it that the cairn of slabs on the headland of Howth is the grave of a fifth-century king, and that the picturesque village of Chapelizod is named for La Belle Iseult, or Iseult of Ireland.

Handsome vistas of classic buildings, the River Liffey, graciously bridged, flowing through the heart of the city, the changing patterns of light on marble or brick create an almost Mediterranean atmosphere. Here one can turn aside and dream, pondering the unseen and the unknown. Here too Dubliners can chuckle over the epigrams of the witty or the antics of the eccentric, for a good anecdote deserves a good audience, and Dublin pubs are filled with both. In this environment the actual can readily become transmuted into the farcical, while legend often seems more real than history, and history itself quickly becomes legend.

The best approach would be at dusk, the late summer sun touching flower and tree until ten or eleven. A "soft" evening it would be, according to the Irish phrase, with only the clouds hurrying. In this light, salmon and claret brick, trim windows and classic porches capture the twilight, and the world of James Malton's aquatint views comes again to life. One understands why Irish literature, from early Christian days to the present, has expressed delight in the moods of nature. The city everywhere lies open to the sky, and in the heart of the commercial districts there is always a vista towards a square, a garden, the river. In 1785 an English visitor expressed his "daily astonishment" at the magnificence of Dublin. As resident Lord Lieutenant, the famous Earl of Chesterfield vowed to make Dublin the most handsome European capital. The hope has nearly been fulfilled. Residential squares, Rutland and Mountjoy on the north, Merrion Square and St. Stephen's Green on the south, with their fenced lawns, reflect one of the most charming features of late Renaissance city design. Dublin is still an eighteenth-century city. The old adage, "England's misfortune is Ireland's opportunity," is as true in architecture and city-planning as it has been in politics. Too poor to afford bad taste, Ireland was spared the horrors of mid-Victorian prosperity, with its efflorescence of "elegance" that blighted so many cities.

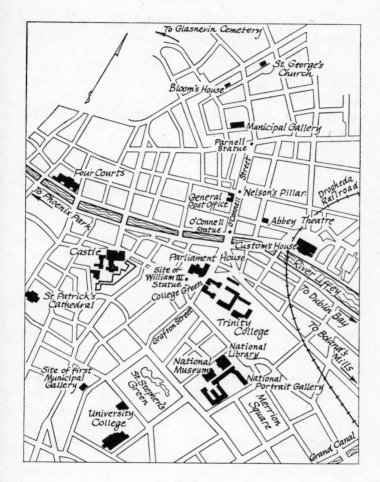

DUBLIN

The street plan itself has a casual symmetry in which classical taste controls the environment without dominating it. Bisected by the neatly channeled river, with the hills of Phoenix Park to the west, and the Dublin Mountains to the south, and ringed elliptically by the old canals, Dublin is a grand town for walking. Distances are not great; there is lots to see; and if you are fortunate enough to find a companionable Dubliner, there is plenty of good conversation.

As one stops for a Guinness, or fish and chips, one might hear the tale of Dublin statues, past and present. You would learn how Justice stood in the yard of the hated Castle, with her back to the people. Also that rain tipped her scales until holes were bored in the saucers. Or you could be entertained by the vicissitudes of King Billy's statue in College Green. Commemorating the defeat of James II at the Battle of the Boyne in 1690, the statue of the stolid king on horseback was erected in the wide thoroughfare. Unfortunately it was thrice vulnerable: first, it was perilously close to the college; second, it was cast of lead; and third, it was in Dublin. Henceforth it became subject to almost constant demonstrations. Twice a year, on the dates of the battle and on the king's birthday, it was publicly honored by Protestants with bells, bonfires, and bottles. It may be suspected that the latter were not limited to the Whigs, for, as Sir Jonah Barrington noted in 1825, Irish political views were something of a puzzle. The Anglo-Irish independent loyalist could drink the healths of the Tory Charles I, the Puritan Cromwell, and the Whig William III on the same evening. This was incomprehensible, unless one assumed that "it was only to coin an excuse for getting loyally drunk as often as possible, that they were so enthusiastically fond of *making sentiments.*" But if the statue was often commemorated, it was just as frequently and more extravagantly shamed—defaced, bombed, tumbled from its pedestal, beheaded! One birthday eve a Trinity student proceeded to paint it black, explaining to the Dogberry on duty that he had municipal orders. In the words of an early guidebook. "It has been insulted, mutilated and blown up so many times, that the original figure, never particularly graceful, is now a battered wreck, pieced and patched together, like an old, worn-out garment." Rebuilding Billy became so frequent a duty that it was said that the horse's raised front left leg was about a foot longer than the right. When last blown up in 1929, the fragments were collected, and later smelted. That is, all but the missing head, which may turn up in some Trinity College attic or in a local junk shop. In the future King Billy's lost head may become the King Charles' head of Ireland!

Then there is little Tom Moore, standing near Trinity College. At one time his head was chopped off in order to elongate his neck by several inches, but the results are still not good. A statue of the daughter of Sir Benjamin Guinness, in St. Patrick's stands in front of a stained-glass window with the text, "I was thirsty and ye gave me drink." A favorite joke among Dubliners is to explain to visitors that Sir John Gray's exploits are to be found on the back of his statue in O'Connell Street. When the curious stop to read, they find the pediment blank. Even Victorianism, so seldom subtle, left a Puckish relic in the monumental fountain of Sir Philip Crampton, now removed. Sir Philip's head peered from the midst of a spire of vegetation, referred to as the "Water Babe" or the "Pineapple," which it did resemble. A closer look revealed that the head was supported on the necks of four most uncomfortable swans, which straddled the basins of water. Not quite so ugly as the Albert Memorial, it looked like the practical joke of an undergraduate. Stephen Dedalus asks his friends ironically whether the statue is epic, lyric or dramatic—and, "if not, why not?" The question goes unanswered. The inscription indicated that the water was intended to be symbolic of:

> *The sparkle of his genial fancy,*
> *The depth of his calm sagacity,*
> *The clearness of his spotless honour,*
> *The flow of his boundless benevolence.*

With their veritable genius for the inappropriate, the Victorians placed the squat figure of their queen directly in the middle of the handsome courtyard formed by the National Library, the National Museum, and the fine Georgian classic façade of Leinster House, the inspiration for our White House. Fortunately she too has been removed. Professor Craig remembers her as "curiously benevolent in her ugliness," but to more disrespectful Dubliners she was once pointedly called "Ireland's Revenge." No wonder that Joyce's fiction is so full of statues—the old mill horse that, forgetting it was pulling a cab, circled King Billy; Robert's epigram in *Exiles*, classing all statues as those with folded arms which seem to ponder, "How shall I get down?" and those, more secure, with outstretched right arms which seem to say, "In my time the dunghill was so high." The cemetery caretaker in *Ulysses* tells the delightful anecdote about the drunk who came to visit Mulcahy's grave and blinked up at a figure of the Savior, exclaiming, "That's not Mulcahy, whoever done it!"

By this time on your tour you have probably met a dozen interesting people and heard more than a dozen stories. You might as well postpone your sight-seeing, more or less indefinitely, and enjoy your companions. Dubliners "believe in being themselves almost to the point of madness," says Michael Campbell in his novel *Peter Perry* (1960). Almost everything is forgiven but dullness. The time of Yeats was one of personalities; indeed, much of the poet's own thought derived from his speculations about his own character, and some of his finest poems were inspired by his appreciation of his friends. The faces are familiar, from descriptions, caricatures, and paintings. As a young man, Yeats was the very portrait of the artist, with abstracted gaze and quick gestures, just as in later years his leonine head, gray hair, and cape made him the "smiling public man" of his magnificent poem "Among School Children." There was the delicate, whey-faced George Moore, the rotund Edward Martyn, and young Jimmy Joyce, tall and slender, insolent and swaggering in his borrowed tennis shoes. "Where but in Dublin," exclaimed James Stephens, "will you meet the author of a ballad in a thousand limericks, each verse of which is better than the last by sheer merit of being worse; or the scholar who could have been a saint but that he preferred to be a wit, and is jeopardizing even that by a lust for the concertina." On the street, "Mr. Yeats will pass like something that has just been dreamed into existence by himself, and for which he has not yet found the precisely fantastic adjective," while the mystic Æ "will jog along, confiding either a joke or poem into his own beard, the sole person in the street who is not aware that he is famous."

Seldom have details of daily life been turned so readily into literary copy, and the ephemeral and local transmuted into the universal. The unconventional surgeon Oliver St. John Gogarty steps into literature strolling down Kildare Street, as he follows the well-known Dublin eccentric nicknamed "Endymion." Gogarty gazes fondly at this lunatic who enters the National Library with bowler on head and cavalry saber in hand, "an odd figure moidered by memories, and driven mad by dreams." From his speculations on the topsy-turvy world of the mentally unbalanced, Gogarty modulates through a sequence of tales, gossip, and opinion which fills many a delightful volume.

In Paris, Joyce interviews a French racing car driver before the Gordon-Bennett races of July 2, 1903; returning to Dublin, he sings in a recital on August 27, 1904. The two experiences are remembered in the stories from *Dubliners*, *After the Race*, and *A Mother*. Yeats is often topical. He celebrates friends and excoriates enemies. Lord Ardilaun offers to make his second contribution to the Municipal Gallery contingent on popular support, and Yeats recalls the unquestioning largesse of Italian Renaissance princes. The tragic events of the wars of liberation evoke responses from many writers, but it was left for Joyce to create an epic from the very eventlessness of what is now one of the most widely known of Dublin days, June 16, 1904, when Leopold Bloom, ridicuolus little Jewish advertising agent, walks unwittingly in the shoes of the mighty Odysseus. From the heroic to the commonplace there was material for song and story, and Dublin's streets and buildings were becoming immortal.

Yeats devoted his life to making himself a poet at the very time that Ireland was becoming a nation. His first collection of verse appeared in 1889. In that year the Irish party rejected Parnell as its leader, and Ireland thereby lost its last hope for independence through constitutional methods. When Yeats died in January, 1939, the present Irish Constitution had been in effect for only one year. It is fitting that Ireland should have produced her first major poet in this period. The coincidence was not entirely accidental, for the experience of Yeats paralleled that of his country, and his questions were hers. Through fifty years he had reflected on national destiny, and in pamphlet, speech, and poem had tried to define the national character. Divided himself, he well bespoke a divided country; by nature timid, he was made bold by opposition. His patriotism was never shallow. If he was at times arrogant and tactless, he always sought a heroic ideal, for himself and for his country.

James Joyce had once taunted Yeats for talking like a man of letters rather than a poet. Yeats never forgot the insult, but in fact he did succeed in becoming both. Since the time of Goethe, few writers have shown such amazing vitality in so wide a range of activities. Certainly few have had the ability to derive from these experiences fresh sources of creative inspiration. What to others might have been distracting interruptions became transformed by the poet's imagination. The power of his writing arises from this grounding in experience, by which his work became a record of his own education as well as a chapter in the nation's history.

Yet the achievements of these years were being accomplished at a cost. Centuries of oppression had left serious scars, and Ireland's quest for cultural and political identity was carried on amid growing discord. Deep-seated religious and temperamental antagonisms were unloosed. Revolution and Civil War were to come, and more than once the future of the country was in doubt. Even today the island remains divided, with six Northern counties retaining their ties to England.

For forty years armed "patriots" roamed about, committing acts of violence. Finally, in February, 1962, the Irish Resistance Movement suspended its activities. Condemnation by the Roman Catholic hierarchy, increasingly severe penalties by the Irish government, and public apathy at last had their effect. Unable to attract recruits or to get financial support, split by dissension, and failing to win a single seat in the general election, the dwindling remnant of what had once been the most romantic, and the most literary (Behan, O'Casey, O'Connor, O'Faolain, O'Flaherty) of modern armies went out of existence.

An artistic flowering is essentially a process of self-discovery, and Ireland's attainment of awareness may owe much of its power to the tragic bitterness of these conflicts. There was a rich inheritance to discover, despite bigotry and rancor. The nationalists and the Gaelic enthusiasts often displayed a doctrinaire narrowness, ready to oppose any English or Anglo-Irish tendencies, but themselves splitting on various questions. The Roman Catholic church, in its long struggle for survival against penal restrictions, had developed a harsh intolerance. These tensions brought forth the usual passion and polemic. Every few years a major crisis developed, beginning with the conflict between patriotic loyalty to Parnell and moral disapproval of his domestic life (see page 115, in this volume).

Yeats once reflected on the public indignation that might be aroused "if any thoughtful person spoke out all his mind to any crowd." Certainly he seemed doomed to be in the midst of controversy, whether among theosophical sects or political groups. More than any of his contemporaries he carried within himself the seeds of these disputes, and it is appropriate that he always stood at the center of the stage, regardless of disrespectful Dubliners who remarked that this was "just what you'd expect of Willie." No matter how highly respected, or bitterly resented, in his many public roles of theatre manager, playwright, publicist, and poet, he was always prey to self-questioning. Few writers convey such a sense of vitality, because few have maintained throughout their lives the personal tension that imparts energy to poetic statement. From his continual inner debates arose one of his most memorable epigrams: "We make out of the quarrels with others, rhetoric, but out of the quarrel with ourselves, poetry." An expert in both modes, he enjoyed dispute as an Irishman should, and wrote poetry of the highest distinction. Each of his literary styles—romantic, satiric, symbolic, realistic—became a vehicle for exalted utterance. To the end of his life, he continued his philosophic quest. Less than a month before his death he summarized his outlook in another notable pronouncement: "Man can embody truth but he cannot know it."

Controversy affected Ireland most drastically in the alienation of her superior minds. Each of the major writers reached a breaking point in relation to his homeland. James Joyce was defiant, although he admitted to being "self-exiled upon his own ego." Before him, George Bernard Shaw and Oscar Wilde had followed the long tradition of Irish genius flourishing abroad, but in 1901 the tide was reversed when George Moore, as full of confidence as conceit, returned home declaring that Ireland was a land of promise. Moore was soon followed by John Millington Synge, who came from Paris in quest of his destined literary material. Even the intransigent Joyce seems to have hoped to return, like the hero of his play *Exiles*. But Synge died in 1909, Joyce never came back to live in Dublin, and George Moore stayed only ten years. In the political turmoil of the "Troubles," and during the early years of the Free State, John Eglinton, Oliver St. John Gogarty, Lord Dunsany, and Sean O'Casey broke away. Yeats and Æ kept faith longest, but both ended their lives in bitter disappointment at modern threats to the Ireland they had dreamed of and in large part created.

The cross-purposes of Irish culture are apparent in the difficulties that Yeats, Æ, and Lennox Robinson encountered in forming an Academy of Letters. Inflammatory sermons and indignant letters attacked the supposedly godless intellectuals. Of those originally invited, Joyce declined, O'Casey ignored the invitation, and the Gaelic enthusiasts Corkery and Hyde refused because of the inclusion of writers using the English language. And the tensions were aggravated among the Irish abroad. The Abbey Players met their loudest opposition in America, and as recently as 1960 an American television program omitted film clips of O'Casey because of protests that the playwright was "a rather shabby expression" of Ireland.

Self-division can destroy an individual or a nation. It can lead to carefree irresponsibility; the stage Irishman as a jolly toper is a caricature of this possibility. It may foster humor, and it has; or at its most profound, it may inspire eloquent protest. One of the spokesmen in Yeats's verse exclaims, "I study hatred with great diligence." Indeed, much of the manly strength of Yeats and Joyce derives from the force of their criticism. What G. K. Chesterton called Ireland's "acrid instinct for judging itself" can be found not only in Shaw, but in Swift and Parnell, Joyce and Yeats. A common trait, surely, except for Æ, perhaps, who had the rare faculty of liking everyone. Yet even he could understand. At the death of George Moore, Æ paid tribute to his old friend, pointing out that in being "remote and defiant," Moore had remained true to his Irish inheritance. As "one of the most talented and unfilial of Ireland's children," he also had benefited his country. His mockery had served to make Ireland "admired and loved" just as much as had "the praise of its patriots." Remembering the value of the critical outlook, Æ said that he himself would remain in Dublin to keep a few heresies alive, and advised Frank O'Connor to do likewise. Opposition could provide creative stimulus: "Take care lest in choosing a nation of free-thinkers you do not destroy the diversity between the world without and the world within which makes you a writer."

There is unfortunately a good deal of truth in James Joyce's diatribe against Ireland as:

> *This lovely land that always sent*
> *Her writers and artists to banishment*
> *And in a spirit of Irish fun*
> *Betrayed her own leaders, one by one.*

But, as Yeats wisely pointed out in regard to Synge, "When a country produces a man of genius he never is what it wants or believes it wants; he is always unlike its idea of itself." The thought can be applied to other writers than Synge, and other countries than Ireland. Æ once pointed a way out of the impasse, writing that "It is of more importance for us to have experience than to have philosophies." In his fine letter of January, 1939, Yeats seems to echo this sentiment: "The abstract is not life and everywhere draws out its contradictions." Then, characteristically, he crowned his meditation with an everyday phrase: "You can refute Hegel but not the Saint or the Song of Sixpence."

In its greatest achievements, the Irish revival reconciled Saint and Song of Sixpence. A strong sense of personal involvement saves it from facile sentimentality and from patriotic rhetoric. It has a sturdy provincialism which nevertheless leads beyond city and country. Fantasy and wit and high seriousness, each the heir of centuries of tradition, join in harmony. At the horizon, the earth touches the sky. Although Synge was accused of demeaning the Irish, his art ennobles those whose contact with sea and soil gives them insight into the universal joys and sorrows of mankind. When the widow Maurya in *Riders to the Sea* survives the last and youngest of her sons, her acceptance recalls the consolations of the Psalmist or the bitter wisdom of Ecclesiastes. Even though none of her family will again ride to the sea. "No man at all can be living for ever, and we must be satisfied." These words, with their simple poetry, were not Synge's, but were actually written to him by an Aran Islander. Yeats and Joyce, starting from different points and using different methods, at last were to meet on common ground. Staying at home, Yeats traveled in imagination to exotic Byzantium, hoping to find the mystic joys of an imperishable art. Remaining abroad,

James Joyce recalled one day of his youth, and revisiting in memory those Dublin streets heard echoes of ancient myth. In the best of modern Irish literature, particular and universal are reconciled, and we pass from the plow to the stars.

II - The Irish Revival

OUT of such stuff as Ireland dreams are made." So George Moore reflected as he considered gracing his native land with his presence after many years in Parisian studios and London salons. It was 1898 or thereabouts, and Mr. Moore was almost ten years late, but then the *avant-garde* does not always live up to its name. By this time everyone in the know had long been in search of the Celtic spirit, even though there was quite some difference of opinion about what it was.

Even today Ireland seems to visitors a land whose enchantment is impossible to resist. The ever-changing skies bathe city and country in a magical aura. The intermittent sunshine, diffused by masses of cloud, touches gray rock and green meadow with vivid patches of light and shade. Color effects are constantly changing in an uncluttered landscape. The copper tones of the peat and the purple of the heather blend with the blue haze of distant mountains. Broken towers and ruined abbeys bespeak the pathos of Ireland's history. Starkly monumental stone crosses, often unfortunately surrounded by cheap and tasteless examples of recent funereal art, stand as proud reminders of the spirit of ancient Irish culture, once the finest in Europe. For Ireland, Cinderella of nations, once enjoyed glory. Her extensive saga literature mingled human and super-natural; stone carving displayed an impressive severe geometrical formality; in manuscript illuminations, decorative design was varied by fanciful and grotesque animal motifs.

Ireland's megalithic monuments are more abundant than those of any other country. Ring forts of earth and stone, frequently called "fairy forts," have been numbered in the thousands. Lake dwellings or crannogs preserved many objects. Treasures of gold and bronze ornaments have been found. Huge tables of leaning slabs, known as dolmens, are common, as are stone circles, although none is as imposing as Stonehenge. By one of the accidents of geography a center of such prehistoric finds is in County Sligo, where the young Yeats spent much time on family visits. Legend and tradition surround the entire area. Sligo, a once proud and prosperous port, is in the heart of Ireland's western coastland. Both sides of Yeats's family came from there, the Butlers and Middletons and Pollexfens and Yeatses so often recalled in his verse. It is glorious country. The bold escarpment of "bare Ben Bulben" stands like the prow of a giant ship jutting oceanward. To the south lies the imposing mass of Knocknarea, topped with an immense cairn, visible for miles, traditionally known as the grave of Queen Maeve, proud heroine of the

Ulster sagas. Luminous, cloud-filled skies shed the radiance which glows in the paintings of Paul Henry and Jack Butler Yeats. Sunlight sparkles on whitewashed houses; gulls soar and scream in the brisk ocean air. A river rushes through the town from Lough Gill, with its wooded isle of Innisfree. On the coastal sands of Lissadell there play "The Little Waves of Breffny" of Eva Gore-Booth's poem. This is a land not for mere men and women but for heroes and goddesses, for poets and painters.

Megalithic monuments are not uncommon in Europe, but only in Ireland do specific legends still cling to them. The romantic historian Standish James O'Grady, father of the revival, pointed out that "In the rest of Europe there is not a single barrow, dolmen, or cist of which the ancient traditional history is recorded; in Ireland there is hardly one of which is not." O'Grady's volumes became sacred scripture to idealistic Irishmen. Æ recalled that in reading them, "It was the memory of race which rose up within me . . . and I felt exalted as one who learns he is among the children of kings."

Ancient heroes and heroines pervade Irish poetry and drama. The tragedy of Deirdre was dramatized by Æ, Synge, and Yeats. Cuchulain was a vehicle for Yeats's imagination from 1892 until 1938. The mighty warrior, archenemy of Queen Maeve, who through treachery was forced to kill his own son in combat and who died fighting the waves, represented to Yeats the nobility of Ireland, the force of passion, the tragedy of love, and the defiance and acceptance of death. The hero's story was told in two poems, "The Death of Cuchullin" (later entitled "Cuchulain's Fight with the Sea") among his earliest, and "Cuchulain Comforted" among the last verse, and in five plays, three of them drastically revised (*On Baile's Strand*, 1903, 1906; *The Golden Helmet*, 1908—as *The Green Helmet* in 1910; *At the Hawk's Well*, 1917; *The Only Jealousy of Emer*, 1919—as *Fighting the Waves* in 1928; The Death of Cuchulain, 1938). Although the tangled threads of the saga are unfamiliar, the sequence of plays, if staged simply and symbolically, and if performed with stylized gestures and musical chant, have a surprising power of evocation.

Of equal importance with O'Grady's redactions of bardic history were the haunting verses collected and translated by Douglas Hyde in *The Love Songs of Connacht* (1893), the sort of book that wins lifelong affection and enthusiasm from its readers. As a Trinity College undergraduate Hyde had astonished a don who inquired whether he knew Irish by his quiet reply: "I dream in Irish." His dreams color the exquisite renderings of the verse, both in poetry and in prose paraphrase. In reading the book Lady Gregory was delighted to learn that "while I had thought poetry was all but dead in Ireland the people all about me had been keeping up the lyrical tradition that existed in Ireland before Chaucer lived." Hyde's prose translations have that enchanting idiom, now so familiar to readers of modern literature in Ireland: "I think it long from me the highroads are," or, "It is courteously, mannerly, beautifully, she said to me." Later to be named "Kiltartan," from the locality near Coole where Lady Gregory collected folklore, the dialect became a self-conscious prose poetry in her plays and in those of Synge. George Moore, who could not abide Lady Gregory, said in *Hail and Farewell* that the idiom "consists of no more than a dozen turns of speech dropped into pages of English so ordinary" as to "appear in any newspaper without attracting attention." It was clever, and malicious, as Moore usually was. When Yeats, who could not abide Moore, turned to writing his own autobiography, he claimed for the style, "Gaelic in idiom and Tudor in vocabulary," a high place indeed.

Dr. George Sigerson compared the discovery of the ancient Irish heritage to finding a buried treasure, and it must have been with considerable pride that members of the newly formed Irish National Literary Society in Dublin heard him advance the claims of this literature, including that of the introduction of rhyme into poetry. In his lecture, reprinted in *The Revival of Irish Literature* (1894) and in his anthology *Bards of the Gael and Gall* (1897), Sigerson outlined some of the varied rhythms of early Irish verse, with its wide use of assonance and consonance, alliteration, and combinations of internal and end rhymes. Except for the pioneer anthology of Charlotte Brooke, the *Reliques of Irish Poetry* (1788), the richness of this literary heritage had been untapped. Miss Brooke had remarked that "It is scarcely possible that any language can be more adapted to lyric poetry," for the language itself "is indeed already music," because of "the smoothness and harmony of its cadences."

The elaborate verse forms have been studied by many scholars, notably by Douglas Hyde, in *A Literary History of Ireland* (1899), and by Robin Flower. As an example of the haunting melodic effects achieved in Irish, Hyde gives a translation of John O'Neaghtan's elegy on the death of Mary D'Este, widow of James II. The second stanza suggests the intricate echoes of the original, although in English the result is something of a jingle:

The Irish Revival

Fair islets of green
Rare sights to be seen
  Both highlands and islands
  There sigh for the Queen.

Meanwhile, a group of eager young men had come under the influence of the newly discovered wisdom of the East, which seemed to confirm their own poetic impulses and to harmonize with the growing Celtic enthusiasms. These adepts gathered on June 16, 1885, to form the Dublin Hermetic Society. William Butler Yeats presided, and the precocious high-school student Charles Johnston read a paper on "Esoteric Buddhism," later published in the new *Dublin University Review*, where Yeats's first poems were appearing. Although it is easy to smile at the paraphernalia of the seance and the ritual of initiation, the fact is that during the 1880's mystical doctrines swept like a brush fire through artistic groups of Paris, London, and Dublin. The Hermetic Society and its successor, the Theosophical Society, provided a philosophic rallying point for the new movement.

There was good reason for the widespread enthusiasm with which the esoteric was sought. In a time when scientific materialism seemed irresistible this lore provided an affirmation of the validity of poetry and the reality of the spiritual world. The artist might once again take the mantle of the seer. Traditions of the ancient and medieval worlds regained significance. The doctrine of correspondences, which even the skeptical Joyce could not resist, suggested the interrelationship of all things past and present, physical and spiritual. An ethereal purification of consciousness replaced the meaninglessness of mechanical progress.

Æ, Yeats's fellow art student in the Dublin School of Art, published his mystical verse in *Homeward: Songs by the Way* (1894). The author explained that he had derived the title from his conception of the soul's return journey to the spiritual realm, on which path through life, "filled ever and again with homesickness, I made these homeward songs."

Reviewing Æ's verse for *The Bookman*, Yeats recalled the "little school of transcendental writers" who had gathered in dingy back rooms some ten years before, composing "many curious and some beautiful lyrics," and spending their time "in battles about the absolute and the alcahest." It must have been an interesting group— Charles Weekes, who withdrew his volume of *Reflections and Refractions* (1893) shortly after publication, but whose fine mystical poems were preserved in anthologies; James Cousins, friend of the young Joyce, an ardent reformer, who published with his wife a charming joint autobiography, *We Two Together* (1950); John Eglinton, blithe revolutionist, "armed not with bombs but with generalizations," the self-styled "Dick Whittington of Idealism."

For several years the theosophists maintained a residence in Dublin, and issued several periodicals. In *Ulysses*, Stephen Dedalus mocks the "yogibogeybox in Dawson Chambers" where disciples gather at the feet of Æ, but he himself was guilty of consulting the master, and, indeed, *Ulysses* and *Finnegans Wake* share, on one plane, an awareness of the eternal and universal spiritual realm. In an introduction to a study of *Three Mystic Poets*, James Cousins identified the major emphases of theosophy, associating them respectively with himself, Æ, and Yeats—

first, the universal brotherhood of humanity (Cousins); second, comparative religion (Æ); third, the occult (Yeats).

Praising Æ's poetry to O'Leary, Yeats's practical afterthought was: "I think we will be able to organize a reception for it." Ever the organizer, Yeats had helped found literary societies in London and Dublin, and was spreading the word of the Celtic Revival in his reviews which were appearing in various periodicals. During these years his literary ideals were comfortably vague. The Celtic dream demanded only the most general commitments, and Yeats had no difficulty in echoing the fashionable enthusiasms of the time. Ireland was, in his opinion, a land of literary promise, its literature still young, and on all sides there were "Celtic tradition and Celtic passion crying for singers." So long as his faith remained untested by experience, it could accommodate pagan as well as Christian themes. Thus he reported in an essay to the Boston *Pilot* in 1891 that "the doctrines I have just been studying in Pater's jewelled paragraphs—the Platonic theory of spiritual beings having their abode in all things without and within us, and thus uniting all things" were related to current Irish thought. Alas, he would soon discover that even though all things might be united, a special problem was posed by the Irish.

For the time being it was conveniently simple to accept prevailing political clichés. Even taste could be temporarily blurred, and Yeats let himself praise mediocre poets: "I knew in my heart that the most of them wrote badly, and yet such romance clung about them, such a desire for Irish poetry was in all our minds, that I kept on saying, not only to others but to myself, that most of them wrote well, or all but well." Yet he was able to forestall the London Irish Literary Society from passing a resolution to the effect that "the time has come" for Ireland to produce a dramatist comparable to Shakespeare. In the midst of his patriotic euphoria he did notice that few could refuse buying "a pepper-pot shaped to suggest a round tower with a wolf-dog at its feet," and that most writers favored "harp and shamrock and green cover" for their volumes. Forthwith Yeats had his label for such enthusiasts—"Harps and Pepper-Pots."

Thus he found himself involved in a rear-guard action against his fellow patriots at the same time that he was opposing such Unionists of Trinity College as Dowden and Mahaffy, even though Dowden was his father's long-time friend. Forced to attack the narrow nationalists who preferred propaganda to art, he held firm even when it meant resisting the patriotic fervor of the fabulously beautiful and unattainable Maud Gonne. The issue was constantly arising, and, as is so often the case in Ireland, it was obscured by political and religious implications. Yeats was making enemies who were to be harmful.

Meanwhile, both his poetry and his pronouncements on Ireland were creating an image of the Celtic spirit, as it was then understood and admired. The Irish can lead in "the imaginative awakening of our time," for theirs had been a long tradition of spirituality and imaginative endeavor. At hand was a vast body of folk belief, a ready reservoir of symbolism. Does Shelley's "over-much cloud and rainbow" not simply reflect his lack of a firm grounding in folklore? In the past Ireland had been notable for its poets, "continually striving to express a something which lies beyond the possibility of expression."

Yeats was soon recognized as the embodiment of Celtic

genius, his poetry an evocation of moods, his subject matter the land and the legends of Ireland, his visionary outlook that of a seer and a dreamer. In 1890 he had published what is still the best-known poem in Irish literature. Although he soon grew tired of its inevitable popularity, Yeats caught, in "The Lake Isle of Innisfree," both the nostalgia for the Irish scene and, almost accidentally, the wavering rhythms of native verse tonalities. From the beginning of his career he had blended the three basic tendencies of the movement: the Celtic, the nationalistic, and the theosophical. It was he who coined the slogan by which the revival was widely known, "the Celtic Twilight." Used as a title to a book of folk sketches, its associations of wistfulness, beauty, and spirituality seemed perfectly appropriate to the new note in the literature of Ireland.

Yeats had just recently written to the aspiring poet Miss Elizabeth White that Irish subject matter helps sincerity and originality, "and gives one less numerous competitors" —advice which Richard Ellmann has cannily called reassuring, since to a young poet "the dangers of being either too sincere or too scheming are about equal." Looking back at this golden age of minor poets, we of a less romantic era can smile at the inflated reputations of now-forgotten writers. One can see how many swans turned out to be geese, and may conclude with John V. Kelleher that it was "a great time for the feeble-minded," when the Celt became a cult, and occult. Then, Professor Kelleher continues, "every common or garden Irish poet began to hear the inaudible, see the invisible, comprehend the unintelligible." Undoubtedly much nonsense was taken seriously, although some of the verse deserves a better fate than it has received. In an age of enthusiasm genius seems to appear daily. Austin Clarke, dean of living Irish poets, recalls that happy time when a man's reputation could be made on one lyric.

To the romantic appeal of ancient Ireland and that of esoteric wisdom was added the tradition of early Christian Ireland, long venerated as the land of saints and sages. Even the bleakest Atlantic headland has its monastery or beehive oratory. Their treasures include not only libraries of manuscripts but beautiful chalices, crosiers, and reliquaries. In the ninth-century Latin verse of an Irishman who became bishop of Fiesole, Ireland was "rich in goods, in silver, jewels, cloth and gold," as well as "benign to the body, in air and mellow soil." This land of "art and men," he continued, was free of bears, lions, and snakes. But not, alas, free of invaders. The tall round tower near the monastery is a stark reminder of the Danish threat. And after the Danes came the English. Meanwhile the country was a loadstone to the devout, who, in the words of the Venerable Bede, traveled thence "either for the grace of sacred learning or a more austere life." Irish scholars and missionaries ventured even beyond the Alps, and such was their prestige that Charlemagne entrusted the development of his educational system to them. It was a land of poets, too; saga and romance and lyric were preserved, and many an early monastic scribe turned from his copying to record that "Pleasant is the glint of the sun today upon these margins," or some like sentiment.

Patriotic pride, nostalgia for a lost culture, the sorrows of defeat, and the pangs of exile make Ireland one of the poignantly loved nations, even though sentiment is often blurred by alcohol in the rendition of Irish song. The obverse of sentiment is fear of criticism. George Bernard

Shaw ridiculed the sentimental notion that Ireland "stands there pure and beautiful and saintly to be eternally oppressed by England and collected for by the Clan"; but after being called the "wild" or the "mere" Irish for centuries, the people are understandably sensitive. Much of the bitterness that Yeats and Synge and Joyce encountered is attributable to this sensitivity. Two centuries before Synge's *The Playboy of the Western World* caused riots at the Abbey Theatre, the Chevalier Charles Wogan pointed out to his friend Swift that "any single blot" in the Irish character "is imputed with great gaiety" by the English to the entire race, "in order to justify their own barbarous proceedings."

Enthusiasm for the Irish language arose from the repressions of neglect and proscription. Legislated against by the English, it declined further with the death or emigration of millions during the famine of the 1840's. Catholics, eligible for government positions for the first time under the Emancipation of 1829, quickly became Anglicized. The National Education Act had also filled the schools with teachers who knew no Irish. Commercial pressures played their part. And so too, unfortunately, did snobbery. The language became a mark of ignorance and a target for ridicule. The bourgeois desire for respectability, "Shoneenism," led to the aping of English customs. The Irish revival thus became a revival of national honor and self-respect.

The language revival followed the pattern established some ten years earlier by the Gaelic Athletic Association, which had spread nationalism throughout the country by encouraging almost forgotten native sports such as hurling. In 1892, at a meeting of the newly formed National

Literary Society, Douglas Hyde, who had already published two volumes of Irish folk tales, spoke on "The Necessity for the De-Anglicising of the Irish Nation." Hyde noted the irony of Ireland's copying the nation she most hated. At the very moment of political awakening, "we find ourselves despoiled of the bricks of nationality." Few addresses have had such an immediate or widespread effect. Within one year the Gaelic League was formed, and many social and political groups followed. O'Growney's Irish primers were sold by the thousands. The calendar was filled with classes, lectures, festivals, concerts, and excursions, all pursued with patriotic fervor.

Ever a gracious gentleman, Douglas Hyde remained above controversy throughout a long and active life, even when he resigned from the presidency of the Gaelic League in 1915 as a protest against its increasingly militant policies. His ability to avoid bitterness won the respect and admiration of Yeats, who, in the midst of a period of estrangement himself, addressed to him the poem "At the Abbey Theatre," inquiring the secret from his friend. Hyde had adopted the pseudonym of "Craoibhin Aoibhin," or "Pleasant Little Branch," the Gaelic of which is, unaccountably to English ears, pronounced "Creevin Eving." Hyde made a charming reply in the next issue of *The Irish Review*, pointing out to his "old companion man-at-arms" that his activities represented "a narrow cult but broader art," and that it was not difficult to keep pace "where men are one at heart."

When the first president of the Irish Republic was chosen in 1939, it was fitting that Douglas Hyde should be selected. His devotion to all that was most traditional in

Irish culture, his long service to his country, and his high personal and intellectual qualities ably qualified him to represent Ireland.

The Gaelic revival raised a myriad of problems. How feasible is it to adopt a national language for a small country dependent on its trade with English-speaking neighbors? How suitable is that language for the expression of modern ideas? How viable are the ancient legends as vehicles for modern literary themes? Can these tales express the nuances of modern sensibility? Finally, how valid are the claims for the Celtic genius?

So much controversy has raged over these questions that only an intrepid or a foolish man would venture an opinion. He would find himself in a veritable Donnybrook, where those deadliest of snipers, the philologists, fire at each other from their ambushes of footnotes. He would hear the age-old insults about Irish laziness and untrustworthiness. Another Swinburne might appear to mock the amateur Celts as "Saxon if not sane." Tired of all this, he might conclude with Rayner Heppenstall that since the word "Celt" has no precise meaning, "Life in these islands might be . . . more sensible if this alibi were wholly abandoned." In his article, printed in the London *Times Literary Supplement*, Heppenstall traced "Celtomania" to *L'antiquité de la nation et de la langue des Celtes* (1703) by a Cistercian monk named Pezron. Pezron described the tribe as the children of Gomer, the eldest son of Japhet, a genealogy which was completed by his translator three years later, who identified the Celts with "our ancient Britons." A dictionary of "Celtick" appeared in Edward Lhuyd's *Archeologia Britannica* (1707). In 1740, William

Stukeley's book on Stonehenge attributed the monument to Celts and Phoenicians, who had preserved the religion and language of the time of Abraham.

The mid-eighteenth century was eager for "noble savages," and few could be nobler than these Biblical vestiges, brave and fair-haired. One of them, Thomas Gray's Welsh hero in *The Bard*, threw himself from the crags to avoid capture. More popular was the melancholy Ossian, whose poems were translated and created by one of the most successful of literary forgers, James Macpherson. In 1760 the young Scottish schoolmaster issued a small volume, *Fragments of Ancient Poetry Collected in the Highlands*. Success was immediate, and there was more poetry where that had come from. The author had forged in his smithy an irresistible blend of Gaelic, Homeric, Miltonic, and Biblical echoes. His settings were equally appealing. The tired blood of rationalism could relax in the funereal gloom of misty glens. Oscar Wilde must have been right in saying that nature follows art as well as it can. If so, the Hebrides were invented by Macpherson:

> *Dost thou not behold, Malvina, a rock with its head of heath? Three aged pines bend from its face; green is the narrow plain at its feet; there the flower of the mountain grows, and shakes its white head in the breeze.*

Grand enough, to be sure, but scarcely superseding Homer, as Goethe once thought. And scarcely Celtic either. Yet what did authenticity matter? Here was Celtic gloom and a heroic home for lost causes. "They came forth to battle, but they always fell," was the famous line, later adopted by Matthew Arnold as an epigraph for his *Study of Celtic Literature* (1867). No better example of circular logic can be found than Arnold's argument: the tone of *Ossian* showed that the Celt was melancholy; the melancholy of *Ossian* showed that the poem was Celtic.

With Ernest Renan and Matthew Arnold the Celt emerges in full glory. Renan's essay on Celtic poetry is a tender elegy for a once powerful race "now concentrated on the very confines of the world," who, turned inward by defeat, had solaced themselves "in taking dreams for realities and in pursuing visions." The essay proved to be unusually popular in the English-speaking world as well as in France, and earned its fraction of an inch in President Eliot's "Five-Foot Shelf" of the Harvard Classics. Renan has been criticized as being a romancer rather than a scholar, and such he admitted himself to be. The *Essais de morale et de critique* (1859), in which the study appeared, constituted a search for an ideal past. "In a time like ours," he wrote, "when every personality of distinction has so little room to move around in, dreaming of an ideal past has become a necessary diversion." In his recent study of the essays, Richard M. Chadbourne has characterized Renan as "an Idealist in the Age of Lead and Tin," whose pessimism was a creative search for a way of life.

Himself of Breton extraction, Renan found these people blessed with the gracious gifts of imagination, chivalry, and religious feeling. "Nowhere has the eternal illusion clad itself in more seductive hues," he exclaimed, and in poetry "no race equals this for penetrative notes that go to the very heart."

Arnold's lectures at Oxford "On the Study of Celtic Literature," delivered in 1865 and 1866, were deeply indebted to Renan, but he made the introverted race a bit more extrovert. As Frederic E. Faverty has noted in *Mat-*

thew Arnold the Ethnologist (1951), the Frenchman's Celts were a *douce petite race naturellement chrétienne,"* but the Englishman's Celts tended "to aspire ardently after life, light, and emotion, to be expansive, adventurous, and gay." To each his own Celt.

Legends die slowly, if ever, when they serve an emotional need. In the case of Celts, it was a national need as well. In his interesting introduction to *The Irish Tradition* (1947), Robin Flower found little evidence for Ossianic gloom in early Irish literature. The poetry reflects the outlook of an active, vigorous people, its main features being "the concrete cast of language, the epigrammatic concision of speech, the pleasure in sharp, bright colour." Thus a quatrain concerning the terrors of barbarian raids is almost imagistic:

> *Fierce and wild is the wind tonight,*
> *It tosses the tresses of the sea to white;*
> *On such a night as this I take my ease;*
> *Fierce Northmen only course the quiet seas.*

A poetry of nature this, of wind in trees, of birds overhead, of sunlight in meadows. But it is not merely descriptive. Mr. Flower points out that these writers evoked a supernal beauty because of their ability to see their environment with eyes "washed miraculously clear by a continual spiritual exercise."

Enthusiasm invites mockery, especially in a divided country. The historian Lecky, reflecting the supercilious attitude of Anglican Ireland, once exclaimed to Lady Gregory, "What silly speeches your Celtic people have been making!" Yet Lecky did subscribe to the support of the Irish theatre. Other Trinity professors were less amenable,

and the opposition of the college to the rising Irish movement continued, with both political and religious motiva-
tions—Lecky himself resigned in protest against the nationalistic activities of Moore, Martyn, and Yeats. In 1899,
Professor Mahaffy testified, during an inquiry into sec-
ondary education, that the revival of Gaelic was "a retro-
grade step, a return to the dark ages." Not content with
this, he added, in a newspaper interview published in the
Dublin *Daily Express* of February 16, 1900, the sneering
suggestion that Home Rulers plead in Irish at Westminster, which "would not only be logical, but would save the
House of Commons from a good deal of incompetent
oratory."

There are amusing anecdotes, of course, which arise
from the ignorance and naïveté of the Gaelic converts.
There was the playwright who said that if he had known
the correct pronunciation of Cuchulain ("Coo-hoo-lin")
he would have characterized that hero entirely differently.
And there was Gogarty's poem "Valparaiso," which, translated into Irish, was accepted as a fine lyric in that tongue,
and thenceforth retranslated into English. George Moore
is the butt of many of these tales, sometimes with his
own acquiescence. He and Yeats reached such an impasse
in collaborating on the play *Diarmuid and Grania* that
Moore, in exasperation. suggested that he write it in
French, and Lady Gregory or Yeats translate it into English, after which it could be translated into Gaelic and
thence to English again! Moore's stories of *The Untilled
Field* first appeared in Irish translations, a year before
the retranslated English version, which the author found
much improved after the "bath in Irish." Three years
earlier, in London, Moore had reflected it was strange

that his country had produced no literature, "for there is a pathos in Ireland, in its people, in its landscapes, and in its ruins." To him the idea of a serious theatre in Dublin seemed "like giving a mule a holiday," and as for the language, he "thought nobody did anything in Irish except bring turf from the bog and say prayers." Very well, then, he would bring culture to Ireland. He made Wildean pronouncements: "I came to give Ireland back her language." He sentimentalized over Breton sailors on the quays. When he asked one whether it didn't "seem odd to hear Celtic speech while you are climbing the ship's rigging high above the stormy seas of Cape Horn?" he was somewhat deflated by the common-sense answer, "Not at all, sir; all of us are Bretons." He had the effrontery to entitle his volume of short stories about Ireland *The Untilled Field* (1903), although, to give the devil his due, they are very fine stories. Learning the language was another matter. No doubt it is difficult; Stephen MacKenna admitted gracefully, "I always swore I'd die a fluent speaker of bad Irish." But when Moore, following in Hyde's footsteps, publicly proclaimed the future of the language, then lamely admitted that he would not learn it himself but would recommend it to his nephews, the satirist Susan Mitchell found her cue. In her delightful verses, "George Moore Comes to Ireland," she impersonates the novelist's swaggering egotism:

> I've puffed the Irish language, and puffed the Irish soap;
> I've used them—on my nephew—with the best results,
>   I hope;
> For with this older, dirtier George, I have no heart to
>   cope.

46

And so on, for several pages. We are also treated to comparable odes on Moore's joining the Church of Ireland, becoming a high sheriff ("hangin' men and women down in Ballaghadereen"), and announcing himself "The priest of Aphrodite." Her volume of satires lives up to the promise of its title: *Aids to the Immortality of Certain Persons in Ireland, Charitably Administered* (1908).

As an impudent college graduate Joyce ridiculed the Gaelic aspect of the revival. In a review of Lady Gregory's *Poets and Dreamers*, printed in the Dublin *Daily Express*, March 26, 1903, "J.J." finds native folklore hopelessly senile. Irish life reverses the normal process of maturing; children, sent to work at an early age, have some sense, but adults seem muddleheaded. If this tendency continues, "little boys with long beards will stand aside and applaud, while old men in short trousers play handball against the side of a house." However right, this was scarcely tactful, especially since Lady Gregory apparently got Joyce the job as occasional reviewer. Buck Mulligan refers to the incident in *Ulysses*, noting that Longworth, the editor, was "awfully sick" about it, and concluding with a gibe at Yeats's rumored financial dependence on Lady Gregory:

> O you inquisitional drunken jew jesuit! She gets you a job on the paper and then you go and slate her drivel to Jaysus. Couldn't you do the Yeats touch?

In one of his multi-level puns Joyce debased the "cultic twalette," yet even he fell under the spell of at least one Irish influence, describing the *Book of Kells* to his old Dublin friend Arthur Power as "the most purely Irish thing we have" and "the fountainhead of Irish inspiration," including that of his own work. And certainly the intricately

allusive language of *Ulysses* and *Finnegans Wake* has its
source in a fantastic richness of imagination similar to that
which, one thousand years before Joyce, found expression in the curiously decorated margins of that treasured
manuscript.

Like his contemporaries, Joyce dreamed of creating
ideals for Ireland. His first consideration of the role of the
artist—his favorite subject—reflects the spirit of dedication in the Dublin of 1904. An essay, "A Portrait of the
Artist," written in January of that year, was rejected by
the editors of the new magazine *Dana*, and has only recently been published (in the Spring, 1960, issue of the
Yale Review). Its peroration envisages a utopian future of
socialistic enlightenment. Even though Ireland remains
"under joint government of Their Intensities and Their
Bullockships," the artist proclaims the goal:

> To those multitudes, not as yet in the wombs of hu-
> manity but surely engenderable there, he would give
> the word: Man and woman, out of you comes the na-
> tion that is to come, the lightening of your masses in
> travail: the competitive order is employed against it-
> self, the aristocracies are supplanted; and amid the gen-
> eral paralysis of an insane society, the confederate will
> issues in action.

Here are the grandiloquence and the vagueness of youth.
Joyce is about to choose exile, and years of frustration are
to leave their mark. Yet the familiar words which conclude
his *A Portrait of the Artist as a Young Man* (1916) still
resound with idealism. Although Joyce's own soured hopes
were beginning to find release in ironic mockery, he
once shared the aspirations of his fictional counterpart,
Dedalus:

I go to encounter for the millionth time the reality of experience and to forge in the smithy of my soul the uncreated conscience of my race.

The excitement of these days can be recaptured in many volumes of reminiscences. Literature really mattered. There was always something new and controversial in the theatre. Dublin newspapers published many articles and letters on literary and political issues. Such editors as T. P. Gill of the *Daily Express* or the hard-hitting D. P. Moran of *The Leader,* as well as the most influential of them all, Arthur Griffith of *The United Irishman* and later of *Sinn Fein*, not only brought artistic and national aspirations to a wide public but exercised a considerable influence in promoting and disseminating opinion. The fullest account remains to be published—the voluminous diary of the architect and playgoer Joseph Holloway, whose 221 manuscript ledgers provide a daily record of Dublin events from 1895–1944. Holloway, the eternal bystander, was always looking in on rehearsals, attending lectures and plays, hearing all the gossip. Whatever the occasion, he wrote it down with Boswellian detail. And few things escaped him. Unafraid of his own opinion, however commonplace it be—and usually was—he regarded dubiously the attempts of Yeats and Lady Gregory to create an art theatre. A good wholesome comedy or melodrama was his cup of tea, and his comments on the notables of the time are refreshingly downright.

In the task of creating a national consciousness, Ireland carried on strenuous debates about literary aims. As one reviews these battles he cannot but be impressed by the persistence with which Yeats maintained his leadership of the Irish movement. The controversy over the play which opened the Irish Literary Theatre in 1899 is a case in point. It may be reviewed here, not with the intent of irritating old wounds, but merely to show the complexities of the socio-politico-religious-literary maze in which the Theatre arose. The intent of Yeats's *The Countess Cathleen* was patriotic, even sentimentally so, with its Faustian theme of the heroine's selling her soul to aid starving peasants. Seldom has any play been so thoroughly reviewed before its performance. With that ineptitude which seems to accompany so many noble experiments, everyone in Dublin had heard of the play and had made up his mind about it before it appeared. One Catholic clergyman attacked it without reading it, and Yeats promptly secured tentative approval by two other church authorities. In a broadside, *Souls for Gold*, Frank Hugh O'Donnell, an old enemy of Maud Gonne's and of Yeats's, charged that the play was blasphemous. Arthur Griffith's *The United Irishman*, while protesting "the merciless methods of Mr. O'Donnell, who tomahawks with the savage delight of a Choctaw," immediately disregarded its own precept of delaying judgment by advising that "we want the poets to inspire and lift up the people's hearts, not to mystify them."

The performance itself made literary history. A group of undergraduates from the Royal University formed a claque to jeer, and submitted a petition to the newspapers—an immature protest which became a brief memory in Joyce's *Portrait of the Artist*. The diarist Holloway dismissed the claque as "twenty brainless, beardless, idiotic-looking youths," but the disturbance was an omen of future troubles. Yeats and the theatre were to be subjected to constant criticism from without and within, for the patriotism of what Joyce termed "the rabblement" does not admit of subtleties. The journal of the Gaelic League attacked the play for being in English, and for being acted and produced under English auspices; it was delighted at the "manful protest of clean, sane, cultured young Irishmen." One Padraic Pearse, later to become leader of the 1916 Rising, feared that the theatre might be more harmful than the despised Trinity College. In his position as "a mere English poet of the third or fourth rank" Yeats was harmless, "but when he attempts to run an 'Irish' Literary Theatre it is time for him to be crushed." Publicists were given to strong words in those days, and actually Pearse was later to be indebted to Yeats for staging amateur performances at the Abbey Theatre for the benefit of the schools he had founded.

The "incomparable" Max Beerbohm, successor to George Bernard Shaw as drama critic for the *Saturday Review*, traveled to Dublin for the performance. Buoyed up by his romantic assignment, "to see and describe the revival of a certain form of beauty" in Ireland, he was brought to earth by the morning newspaper, which reminded him that he was in the land, not merely of tears and dreams, but of wigs on the green. Yeats's verse seemed "made to be chanted," and even though most of the cast were "terrified amateurs," the stage cramped and the scenery tawdry, Beerbohm felt that "a beautiful play was being enacted."

The argument was only beginning, and the confused directions of opinion can be seen in the pages of Griffith's newspaper, which wound up agreeing with no one, not even with itself. It could not join "the hollow shout" of approval from the Irish *Independent*, nor, on the other hand, could it assent to the Gaelic League's charge that only plays in Irish were acceptable. The narrowness of the objectors was apparent, yet the editor could not "condemn the warm-souled youths," who, however warm-souled, had yet "mistaken what Mr. Yeats distinctly stated to be a purely symbolic play for a pseudo-historic one." Even so, the story is not concluded, for the next week's issue contained an attack on Yeats by Fred Ryan. The author should have either ignored his opponents or "proclaimed his right to think for himself," instead of securing the approval of two Catholic priests—"Really, we are too timid." And as for the young men, Ryan was not so hopeful as the editor: "We know these young men—the people who are always prepared to throw the example of the dead pioneers at the heads of the living ones," but who would have been the first to attack the leaders of other days.

Looking ahead to November, 1901, we see Arthur Griffith picking up an essay by James Joyce as a stick to beat the censors, though disagreeing with the young Royal University graduate's attack on the theatre. In reviewing *The Day of the Rabblement*, privately printed after its rejection by the college magazine, *St. Stephen's*, Griffith hoped for a "large sale, if only to convince blooming Censors and budding Censors that this is the twentieth century, and that it is a holy and wholesome thing for men and women to use the minds God gave them." Indeed, "why the Censor strove to gag Mr. Joyce is to me as profound a mystery as why we grow Censors at all . . . . Turnips would be more useful." Yet Joyce himself, in Griffith's opinion, "adopts a rather superior attitude," and, since sneering at Yeats, Moore, and Martyn had become so common, "one wonders why Mr. Joyce should fall so low." It seems that "those who write and talk so glibly about what the Irish Literary Theatre ought to do and ought not to do"—that is, all but the staff of the *United Irishman*—"have no idea of the difficulties" that a theatre meets. The editor concludes with an injunction: "*Patience,* Mr. Joyce, and your desires for the masterpieces may have fulfillment." Thus ends one of the earliest press notices Mr. Joyce received.

Although tempers undoubtedly ran high at times, discussion of the new literature made for lively interest. Some of the issues are still relevant. Problems of national literature and of popular art were raised; the rival demands of realism and symbolism were voiced. The aesthetics of realism, deriving from Wordsworth and Tolstoy, centered art in human experience. Symbolism claimed sanction as an expression of man's eternal spiritual aspirations. Two small volumes emerged from such debates. *Literary Ideals in Ireland* (1899) included essays by John Eglinton, Yeats, Æ, and William Larminie which had appeared in the literary columns of the Dublin *Daily Express.* The similarly named *Ideals in Ireland* was edited by Lady Gregory two years later.

John Eglinton had opened the first discussion by expressing doubts concerning the suitability of Irish legend for contemporary drama. He suggested that ancient myths "obstinately refuse to be taken up out of their own environment," and that what is needed for a vital literature is simply a strong interest in and capacity for life. In reply, Yeats made an eloquent defense of poetic idealism. He predicted that the current "renewal of belief" would increasingly free the arts from practical concerns: "I believe that all men will more and more reject the opinion that 'poetry is a criticism of life' and be more and more convinced that it is a revelation of a hidden life." Indeed, the arts may eventually replace religion, becoming "the only means of conversing with eternity left to man on earth."

Actually Eglinton was not far behind Yeats in his respect for the arts. He concluded with an assertion of the artist's independence that seems to have appealed to Joyce, then a first-year student at the Royal University (now University College, Dublin). "In all ages," Eglinton wrote, "poets and thinkers have owed far less to their countries than their countries have owed to them." Joyce remembered the thought some fifteen years later. In Trieste, on the eve of World War I, he wrote the sixteenth chapter of *Ulysses* (one of the first to be put on paper). It is after midnight, and the weary poet Stephen Dedalus is bored by his garrulous companion Leopold Bloom. The disillusioned young man hears, "over his untasteable apology for a cup of coffee," the tiresome words "patriotism," and "work," and "Ireland." Stephen bewilders his well-meaning companion with his reply, "But I suspect . . . that Ireland must be important because it belongs to me."

Discussion is not literature, of course, and one may regret that Yeats found it necessary to descend to the arena so often for the purposes of explanation or defense, even though it was to prove a firm foundation for his creative effort. Manifestoes are often important preludes, and in Ireland they were part of the search for an inheritance. The continuity of its own culture had been drastically severed, and for several centuries Ireland remained a provincial outpost. Irish artists and men of letters had inevitably been swallowed up by the dominant English tradition, and one of the necessary steps for the reversal of that tendency was the establishment of a rival culture. In this quest for identity, the factors of race, language, religion, and nationality played important roles—a difficult task, indeed, yet not without compensations. The lack of any strong tradition left Ireland free to respond to the currents of contemporary life, and the work of Joyce and Yeats, while rooted in native experience, is far from provincial.

Yeats's poetic achievement has absorbed the attention of literary historians at the expense of a consideration of his pioneering work as a critical exponent of symbolism. His interpretations of Blake and Shelley and his explorations into the significance of the creative process are landmarks in modern criticism. Much of his early work remains uncollected, but the essays in the 1903 volume, *Ideas of Good and Evil*, contain classic statements of the value of symbolism.

The Abbey Theatre and its predecessors have been Ireland's mother of genius, sometimes her bad boy, and sometimes her too respectable matron. The story has been told by many of the major participants, with more or less personal bias—by Lady Gregory and by George Moore in his reminiscences, by Yeats in his autobiography and in the essays collected as *Plays and Controversies* (1923). There have, indeed, been almost as many controversies as plays. There were quarrels over organization, over play selection and direction, over touring policy. And the public was sometimes better heard than the cast, notably in the famous week in January, 1907, when Synge's *The Playboy of the Western World* ran for night after night amid jeers and catcalls. There were episodes and escapades, such as Yeats's sly publication of *Where There Is Nothing* in

55

Griffith's *United Irishman,* which George Moore would be powerless to attack, for fear of appearing unpatriotic.

In view of all this, the opening prospectus has a somewhat ironic ring today, with its expectation that "We hope to find in Ireland an uncorrupted and imaginative audience trained to listen by its passion for oratory." The theatre planned to produce "Celtic and Irish plays," which, regardless of quality, would be written "with a high ambition." In her account of *Our Irish Theatre* (1913), Lady Gregory smiled at the use of the word "Celtic." Confessing that "I myself never quite understood the meaning of the 'Celtic Movement,'" she gave her own interpretation: ". . . to persuade the Scotch to begin buying our books, while we continued not to buy theirs."

In spite of vicissitudes, the Abbey Theatre did bring poetic drama and poetic acting to a country which had long been forced to subsist on a diet of road shows from England, with their tired and tried slapstick and melodrama. The Theatre's powers of revival have been amazing. Time and again it has been pronounced dead, only to turn up with more gifted playwrights. George Moore and Edward Martyn retired early, but they were immediately followed by Synge and Lady Gregory. The completely inexperienced mistress of Coole Park revealed an unexpected gift for comedy, and her sketches of Irish life have been among the Abbey favorites. The Theatre might have seemed doomed at the time of Synge's death in 1909, but then appeared Lord Dunsany and Lennox Robinson, and after them, Sean O'Casey.

Yeats was active in every phase of the dramatic movement. He wrote some of the finest poetic and symbolic plays of this century, and, ever the expert publicist, reiterated the ideals of the literary theatre in essays and speeches. He raised money for the company by lectures and private readings, and often had to undergo criticism as a snob or an English sympathizer for his appearances in country houses. Exhausting and time-consuming as these activities must have been, they gave to the poet a grounding in human experience that brought the solidity of life to his poetry.

During the twenty years before the outbreak of war in 1914, Irish poetry was attracting as much attention as the Irish theatre, and Yeats, early recognized as the master, was considered to be first among many near equals in lyric poetry. The truth is that an amazing amount of good verse was written. As E. V. Lucas exclaimed to Stephen Gwynn regarding Æ's anthology of younger poets, the *New Songs* of 1904, here were "eight people I never heard of, and they all write so confoundedly well!" A great number were indeed writing confoundedly well. For twenty years slim volumes of verse were appearing each season, and the harvest was periodically gathered in collections, one of the earliest of which had been edited by Yeats in 1895.

These anthologies do not exude the expected musty odor of plush and faded cretonne. To dip into them is to experience a delicate music, evocations of mood which are now out of fashion to be sure, but which still seem far superior to the clichés of Victorian sentiment. Minor but far from mediocre, this poetry deserves a small niche in literature. When he reviewed Douglas Hyde's translations of the *Love Songs of Connacht* (1893), Yeats had spoken wistfully of the freshness of these expressions of sorrow or ecstasy by forgotten Gaelic singers. He had closed the book "with much sadness," aware as he was of the loss of innocence which separated that early time from the present. "The soul then had but to stretch out his arms to fill them with beauty," but now "we stand outside the wall of Eden." To readers of a later day the early years of the century seem to retain something of the pastoral simplicity for which Yeats was even then yearning.

The sapphire and amethyst hues of Æ's verse have faded, and little of his once greatly admired poetry retains vitality. He confessed to Sean O'Faolain that he wrote as though he were actually "on the slopes of death," and that he was deeply gratified when it brought comfort to others. His sweetness and spirituality are apparent, and one may only regret that his visions are so intangible. Few of his lines are memorable, largely because they seem to dissolve into the insubstantiality of dream. One recalls

> *Our hearts were drunk with a beauty*
> *Our eyes could never see*

and wishes that he could recall more. His meditation on "Reflections" comes closer to actual experience, arising as it does from the blue surface of an Irish lake and leading to a consideration of the borrowed grandeur of man, "with mirrored majesties and powers." More specific is "An Irish Face," a study of the lines of sorrow imprinted on the features of a child:

> *And dreaming of the sorrow on this face*
> *We grow of lordlier race.*

Becoming transformed by "a deep adoring pity," we are thereby made into "what we dream upon."

We may also regret, as did Æ, that so little of the lighter, human side of his nature came to be expressed in his poems. Lady Gregory mentions his "humbugging verses" which teased James Stephens, but in his volumes of poetry Æ's official mood of high seriousness seldom allowed him to show the twinkle in his eye.

Modern taste is better satisfied with the Franciscan spirituality of Katherine Tynan Hinkson's views of natural beauty, or the peasant simplicity of Padraic Colum's rustic characters—plowman and cattle drover and crone, all instinct with humanity; the old woman of the roads with her longing for a neat house with pendulum clock and gleaming china; the threadbare scholar of the hungry forties, forgetful of political urgencies, teaching by rushlight, his reward years hence being

> *. . . in rustic speech a phrase,*
> *As in wild earth a Grecian vase.*

The last line, we are told in *Ulysses*, was admired by Yeats when Æ's *New Songs* appeared.

Akin to the characters in Colum's verse is "The Old Woman" of Joseph Campbell, beginning with the unpretentious lines:

> *As a white candle*
> *In a holy place,*
> *So is the beauty*
> *Of an aged face.*

Campbell's dancer, with the characteristic Irish combination of intricate footwork and motionless arms and mask-like face, takes on significance as an image of Ireland. Mention of the dance leads to the roguish gaiety of Synge. Himself a fiddler and a lover of peasant Ireland, Synge's "Beg-Innish" deserves to be remembered for its rollicking rhythms:

. . . .

> *Four strings I've brought from Spain and France*
> *To make your long men skip and prance,*
> *Till stars look out to see the dance*
> *Where nets are laid to dry.*

One hurries regretfully past Winifred Letts and his extravagant praise of "The Kerry Cow," which, we are told, deserves to rank "with the horse of Troy and Oisin's hounds and other beasts of fame," to come to Seumas O'Sullivan's quiet evocations of street scenes in north Dublin, where funerals pass day after day, and the organ-grinder or lamplighter alone disturb the somnolent atmosphere of decay. Thomas MacDonagh, scholar and patriot as well as poet, captured the rough humor of peasant life in "John-John," the wife's farewell to her husband, a vagrant tinker, gone three years:

> *Oh, you're my husband, right enough,*
> *But what's the good of that?*
> *You know you never were the stuff*
> *To be the cottage cat.*

And so a cheery "God bless and keep you far, John-John!" There is that notable poem of the 1916 Rising, Dermot O'Byrne's ballad, which excoriates Dubliners even more than the English, for it will be the corner boys, who, surviving

> *With desert hearts and drunken eyes*
> *We're free to sentimentalize*
> *By corners where the martyrs fell.*

Neither of the erstwhile pals, Gogarty and Joyce, put much of their natural exuberance into their classically molded poems, although each was responsible for notoriously unprintable verse. Gogarty's lyrics suggest Roman epigram; Joyce's, the songs of Ben Jonson. And Gogarty is especially felicitous in penning memorable lines: "If medals were ordained for drinks," or "Win to Fame through indolence." He too treated the myth of Leda, "all with wonder stirred." Best, perhaps, is his stoic "Non Dolet," with its commanding opening, "Our friends go with us as we go," and its noble final acceptance of death, "Nor, after Caesar, skulk in Rome."

Meanwhile, a number of painters were securing for Ireland a small but significant place in the arts. The veteran among native artists was Nathaniel Hone (1831–1917). After a brief career as an engineer, Hone studied and worked in France for seventeen years, returning to reside in the country north of Dublin. He had been closely associated with Manet, and applied techniques of the Barbizon School to Irish landscapes, using patches of pigment to bring out the highlights of stony fields and country roads.

John Butler Yeats's portraits of the major figures in the revival retain much of the graciousness of Dublin at the turn of the century. At the suggestion of Hugh Lane, the poet's father left London in 1902 and undertook an extensive series of portraits in oil and crayon. Most of literary and artistic Dublin sat for him. Years later Susan Mitchell, one of his subjects, recalled his manner of painting: "The brave, tall figure, brush in hand, advancing on his canvas with great strides . . . putting on touches with the ardour of one who would storm a fortress," and, of course, "talking enchantingly all the time, his whole nature in movement." His rooms on St. Stephen's Green, more salon than studio, were filled with friends. He kept so busy chatting that his portraits were produced very slowly; moreover, as his son recalled, his impressionable mind was always open to afterthoughts, so that everything he did was constantly being retouched.

A high level of competence and skillful use of the techniques of genre and portraiture was reached by the academy painters Sir John Lavery (1856–1941), Walter Frederick Osborne (1859–1903), and Sir William Orpen (1878–1931). Sir John Lavery painted Arthur Griffith, "staring in hysterical pride" as Yeats says in his poem on the Municipal Gallery, and the even more striking treatment of de Valera's craggy face, a study in tones of gray which brings out the sitter's serious introspective mood. He was also responsible for the political illustration mentioned by Yeats, the blessing of the tricolor.

Robert Gregory's few pictures indicate that Yeats was probably right in judging him "a great painter in the immaturity of his youth." Gregory's almost surrealistic landscape of Coole, with its bare outlines and subdued coloring, must have been in Yeats's mind when he wrote in his memorable elegy, "We dreamed that a great painter had been born/ To cold Clare rock and Galway rock and thorn."

Jack Butler Yeats, like his brother, developed his art through well-defined stages. His early silhouetted figures of tinkers and fishermen have the boldness of primitive woodcuts, and it was in keeping with this style that he illustrated the ballad broadsides published by his sisters' Cuala Press. Pastel tones were used in the landscapes of the middle period; then, in a late burst of creative vitality similar to his brother's, he turned to the expressionistic exploitation of strong colors and undefined forms. But whatever the technique, his never-faltering love of humanity is apparent. In the words of Thomas McGreevy, he painted the Ireland that matters.

V - Personalities

FROM the time of Barrington to that of Brendan Behan, Dublin has cherished personality. The city is small enough for individuals to be known as individuals. People are news, and the only thing worse than being talked about is not being talked about. Everyone worth knowing is sure to turn up in the course of the day, at the theatre or the library or the newspaper offices and pubs. In Irish novels and reminiscences they are to be found, those eccentric dons from Trinity, the ready-witted advocates, the worldly scholars, the poetic medical students. Long after they are gone their words are remembered and their presence felt. There was the eighteenth-century don, Jacky Barrett, whose antics are still relished. Although an outstanding Orientalist, he was such an extraordinary hermit that he reached middle age before he knew what sheep looked like. His expression of delight at seeing "live mutton" was equaled only by his appreciation of the sea, which he described as "a broad flat superficies, like Euclid's definition of a line expanding itself into a surface." He once made the practical suggestion that Trinity College dispose of some rubbish by digging a hole in which to bury it. When asked what was to be done with the earth taken out of the hole, he came up with the idea of digging another hole for it!

Visitors to Dublin in the early years of this century were quick to notice the charm of the people they met. H. W. Nevinson wrote of the "varied and lovable" men and women "who have given a grace and poignant interest to Dublin life such as I have found in no other city." Nevinson's descriptions of his visits in 1900 and 1903, with their brief vignettes of Dr. Sigerson, Æ, O'Leary, and others, are among the most rewarding pages of his autobiographical *Changes and Chances* (1923). He tells of Maud Gonne, "lovely beyond compare," and of Yeats, "very much the poet," who "talked well and incessantly, moving his hands a good deal, and sometimes falling into a natural chant."

In *Dublin Explorations, by an Englishman* (1917), Douglas Goldring gave a more detailed and more critical account of Dublin's intellectual life. Political discussion was free and unprejudiced, a refreshing change from the timidity and conventionality of English conversation. On literary and artistic matters, however, "the value of the opinions expressed" seemed to him rather limited and commonplace, "rarely on a level with the authority and brilliance with which they were delivered." He found his tour of the National Portrait Gallery less an artistic experience than a delightful visit with interesting people: "All the Irish great seem to have been men who were spendthrift of their personalities, giving most generously to the social life of their time all that they possessed of wit, of creative energy, intelligence, fantasy, or charm."

Seldom have personalities played so important a role in literature as in the Ireland of Yeats. One thinks of George Moore's reminiscences and of Joyce's *Ulysses*; but no Irish writer hesitated to use himself, his friends, or his enemies, as copy. The Dubliner's gift of phrase made these verbal portraits as memorable as the familiar oil paintings and drawings of celebrities, many of them gifts by Hugh Lane, the art connoisseur and nephew of Lady Gregory.

A sensationally successful art dealer, Lane was a center of controversy in death as in life. He was suspected of selfish motives when he urged Dublin to buy masterpieces, and even when he offered his own collection to the city provided a suitable gallery be built. Obviously the best-qualified candidate for the curatorship of the National Museum, he was passed over in favor of the Papal Count George Plunkett, thereby provoking the first of Yeats's topical satiric poems, "An Appointment," published in 1909. The ironies of history decreed that Plunkett's son was to be among the martyrs of the Easter Rising, and that the Count himself was to serve a prison sentence as a patriot and to become the first Sinn Fein candidate to win a parliamentary seat, early in 1917. Lane died in the sinking of the *Lusitania* in 1915, and thenceforth his unwitnessed codicil, bequeathing thirty-nine paintings to the Dublin National Portrait Gallery, was disputed. The London National Gallery, to which the pictures were first given in the will, kept them until, in 1960, a reciprocal loan plan was instituted. The last years of Lady Gregory's life were saddened by her failure to gain the pictures for Ireland.

Even without the disputed pictures, Lane's benefactions

were impressive, including more than sixty paintings of the traditional schools. Among them were canvasses by Bordone, Strozzi, and Poussin which provided images for Yeats's poetry. In addition, Lane, inspired by Lady Gregory's enthusiasm, commissioned John Butler Yeats, William Orpen, and others to paint portraits of Irish celebrities. These pictures reveal strong features, in which vigor and sensibility are blended. Seeing them, one understands the impact of these writers, actors, and political leaders on Irish culture, and senses the distinctively Irish and Anglo-Irish flavor of their personalities. In the eager gaze of Æ as he peers through his spectacles Count Markievicz creates an impression of this famed host who was as keen to hear the views of others as he was to express his own. J. B. Yeats caught in the relaxed figure of Synge, arms crossed, a faintly perceptible smile on his lips, the earthy humor and tragedy of his plays. Epstein's bold head of Lady Gregory conveys her matronly strength. In the pencil sketch by J. B. Yeats the young poet Padraic Colum is wistfully meditative. Mancini's bold use of chiaroscuro was admired by Synge, who, Yeats tells us in his poem on the Municipal Gallery, thought the Lady Gregory portrait the finest since Rembrandt. Even better is his monumental canvas depicting the sensitive and aristocratic figure of Lane himself.

Portraits of the Fay brothers of Maire Ni Shiublaigh and Moira O'Neill, as well as Robert Gregory's striking depiction of Arthur Sinclair in cavalier costume, from the Abbey Theatre collection, remind us of the important role played by the actor in the development of the Irish revival. The tradition continues. The work of Hilton Edwards and Michael MacLiammoir in the Gate Theatre has been memorable, and the current tour de force of Mac-

Liammoir, the most gifted of living Irish actors, in his one-man recreation of Wilde's life and times, has deserved the plaudits it has won in Europe, South America, and the United States. For more than two hours he holds his audiences as he recreates the personality of the most famed of Dublin wits and summarizes his meteoric rise and even more sensational nemesis.

At every stage of his long career William Butler Yeats looked the part he was playing, from the youthful aesthete his father painted in 1900, in dark jacket, with unruly forelock, pince-nez, and flowing tie, to the mocking old man in the 1934 portrait by Augustus John, in shirt sleeves with open collar, his white hair blowing in the wind.

In these Dublin collections—the Municipal Gallery, the National Portrait Gallery, and the Abbey Theatre portraits—are to be found the true images of Yeats's Dublin. No one, however, seems to have been able to capture the statuesque beauty of Maud Gonne, the inspiration of a dozen immortal poems. Sir William Orpen's striking portrait of Captain John Shawe-Taylor, in scarlet coat, conveys the same impression as did Yeats in his essay on this gallant man. His handsome appearance was not an idle consideration, Yeats wrote, for in some men "good looks are an image of their faculty." Like the commanders whose features were admired by ancient historians, such men have the power of sudden decision, like hawk or leopard, "as if their whole body were their brain."

The exaltation of the personal carries over into the realms of thought. The lack of any central cultural tradition in Ireland prompted a free play of individuality and a refreshing originality, but its perils can be seen in the constant tendency toward the subjective and the esoteric.

Yet however far the artist's quest leads into the irrational and the occult, it seems eventually to return to the world of men. Æ describes his visions in paintings and poems, but he finds these visions applicable to his other careers of economist and molder of public opinion. Yeats transmutes his cabalistic speculations into concrete symbols of sword and fire and golden bird, and the world's poetry is thereby enriched. One striking exception is the later work of Joyce, whose contrapuntal, polylinguistic *Finnegans Wake* demands a dozen pages of exegesis for each page of text.

Writers were saved from the dangers of private delusion by the practical affairs in which they participated, and by the constant interplay of personalities in Dublin. The popular "at-homes" provided both sounding boards and testing grounds. Seldom have there been such gatherings of talent, at least since the days of Johnson's Club. The quality of these evenings can never be retrieved, but something of their atmosphere has been preserved. Most brilliant of all Dublin talkers seems to have been the journalist and self-taught classicist Stephen MacKenna. The astonishing variety of his conversation is still remembered, ranging in subject from poetry to politics—he had reported the abortive Russian Revolution of 1904–1905—and in tone from the splendor and dignity of Yeats to the gay fantasy of James Stephens.

As famous as the MacKenna Saturday evenings were the Sundays at Æ's and the Mondays at the home of Yeats. Most spectacular of all were the monthly parties held by the venerable Sarah Purser in the grand ballroom of her Georgian mansion. Although she was Shaw's senior by almost twenty years and had seemed old to Yeats as a boy, she outlived Yeats and maintained to the time of her death at the age of ninety-five the reputation of being the wittiest woman in Dublin as well as one of its most distinguished artists. Her sensitive portraits of the major literary figures are comparable to those by John Butler Yeats.

In *As I Was Going Down Sackville Street*, Gogarty describes one of his own Fridays at the time of the Civil War. Ignoring the machine-gun fire in the street, Æ expostulated imperturbably, holding the attention of the stalwart military hero of the Free State, Michael Collins, who had been tracked by spies to the very doorstep. Although subject to ambush at any moment—he was murdered a few weeks later—Collins maintained his cool gallantry, even reaching for a pad to take a note. But Æ's mystic speculations were beyond the General's ken. Collins' voice rang out in direct question: "Your point, Mr. Russell?" The mood was shattered. In his multiple roles as host, proud friend of Collins, and *littérateur*, Gogarty was, for the moment, almost thrown off balance. But he recovered sufficiently to let Collins depart for a place of hiding, to urge Æ that the group was still avid for astral wisdom, and, at the end of the evening, to apologize to the American college girls who were among the guests, explaining that though his home was ever open to patriots and to friends, it was, above all, "a house for artists and not for lecturers, readers, preachers, teachers or people with points." As an artist, Æ communicated himself, not points.

The value of Monk Gibbon's recent memoir of Yeats may arise largely from the resentment which it expresses, for none of the biographical studies of the poet convey the unfavorable impression he sometimes created in Dublin during his life. On his return home from his teaching post abroad, Gibbon always found it "an intoxicating experience to come back to Dublin and its great talkers." Himself Irish, Gibbon was not content to listen. He felt impelled to question, and to contradict. And he sensed, perhaps wrongly, that Yeats would entertain no opposition, speaking ex cathedra on all issues, and showing no interest in contrary views. T. Sturge Moore once made a distinction between the "provocative truculence" of the public Yeats and his "seductive delicacy" in private. If this be true, Gibbon seems to have seen only the public man. The dramatic frankness of Gibbon's account somewhat alleviates its bitterness, but the slurs which the young man suffered, or imagined, have apparently rankled for years. He suppresses neither his personal resentment nor his respect for Yeats, and one puts down the book with a vivid picture of both the greatness and the smallness of Yeats—his mastery of words and ideas, his occasional lack of mastery of his own vanity.

For Gibbon, evenings at Æ's were entirely different, since "one never went away with the feeling that one had talked too much, for everyone there talked too much." The crowded Sunday evenings were lively and democratic. Olivia Robertson recalls how the poet "shed over those who knew him the beautiful atmosphere of blue and gold tranquillity that one finds in his paintings." His friend and neighbor Constantine Curran has written that "the variety of his conversation was a Dublin proverb, ranging over philosophy, economics and the arts." John Eglinton quoted a visitor's impression of "this big bearded man" who, surrounded one evening by sophisticated talkers, "remained silent and ruminative, only occasionally interrupting to state in simple quiet words so wise that in a moment they annihilated the brilliant twaddle." As he said good-by to this "kindly, humorous, wise man, of enormous tact and great toleration," the visitor "could not but feel as he took my hand that I had for some few hours been in the presence of a man of noble mind and strange, disturbing genius." Ernest Boyd has described the "great rhythmic torrent" of Æ's conversation, with its emotional depths and spiritual overtones.

Æ had an incredible memory, and at one time was reputed able to recite not only all his own verse but everything that his friend Yeats had written. We must not let the image of the seer blind us to the fact that he was a man of affairs. For twenty-five years his was the most articulate voice of the national conscience. His periodicals, *The Irish Homestead* and later *The Irish Statesman*, constantly measured current political events against his own high standards. He answered Kipling's inflammatory attack on Irish Catholicism. When the newspaper owner William Murphy was breaking the Dublin transport strike of 1913, Æ's "Open Letter to the Masters of Dublin" arraigned the capitalist with the vehemence of a Hebrew prophet:

> You may succeed in your policy and ensure your own damnation by your victory. The men whose manhood you have broken will loathe you, and will always be brooding and scheming to strike a fresh blow.

Three years later he traced the tragic Easter Rising to the ill will of employers during the Great Strike: "It was Labour supplied the passional element in the revolt." Like Yeats, he could accept the "terrible beauty" that was born in Easter week, although he felt that the Devil was loose in Ireland during the Civil War, with "crazy Gaeldom" uncontrolled. As the new country seemed to develop the same old politicians, he was finding it more and more difficult to remain loyal. Left alone by his wife's death and his son's moving to America, however, at last he decided that it was time "to break up the mould of mind in which I was decaying." Even so, he parted with his paintings and his books and left home and friends in a characteristic mood of optimism and indignation: "I think the change will reinvigorate me, and it will be a relief to get away from Ireland in its present mood, which is one of smugness."

Throughout his life, Æ enjoyed an almost universal love and respect. George Moore even forgot himself—*mirabile dictu*—long enough to make Æ the most attractive figure in his *Hail and Farewell* (1911–14). To Moore, he seemed a man from fabled Arcady, with "the mind of Corot in verse and prose," whose pastels conveyed "a spiritual seeing of the world." Arch-mocker and egotist as he was, Moore could not ridicule a man whose 'gray pantheistic eyes . . . looked so often into my soul with such a kindly gaze." The kindly gaze embraced younger writers too. It was Æ who opened his journals as well as his home to new talent, and who published lyrics by Padraic Colum, Eva Gore-Booth, Susan Mitchell, and others in his anthology *New Songs*. Joyce's disappointment at not being included is apparent in the discussion of the book in *Ulysses*, but again it was Æ who first published Joyce's fiction, three of the *Dubliners* stories appearing in *The Irish Homestead* in the latter half of 1904.

Yeats and Moore gibed at Æ's protégés with such expressions as "Russell's poultry-yard" or his "canaries." Yeats was honest enough to admit his jealousy of the personal popularity of his former schoolmate and fellow poet. He suspected Æ's salon to be the main source of opposition to his control of the Abbey Theatre, even though it was the "chief centre of literary life in Dublin." A shrewd appraisal of this rivalry by Mrs. Yeats is probably correct. Yeats himself quoted it in a letter to Dorothy Wellesley: "My wife said the other night, 'Æ was the nearest to a saint you or I will ever meet. You are a better poet but no saint. I suppose one has to choose.'"

As ugly political realities began to tarnish ideal visions of Ireland, Æ's reputation started to wane, and later visitors were not so much entranced by the evenings on Rathgar Avenue. They could note the little drama of preparation before the oracle spoke. They accused him of loving to hold the floor, a charge to which few Dubliners could plead innocent. O'Casey, for one, was immune to Æ's charm. To him the aging seer was "Dublin's Glittering Guy." In his two visits O'Casey had heard nothing but a "spate of blather." Æ was as much a humbug in his monotonous and vague poetry as in his romantic and amateurish paintings. O'Casey made no attempt to be fair in his judgment, and one can scarcely imagine a greater disparity than that between O'Casey and his target—in background, character, or outlook.

The salons of Yeats and Æ constituted rival camps. The history of literary affinities and antipathies in Dublin has the complexity of Balkan politics. Alliances could be charted by noting the roles of the major figures. Throughout his life Yeats remained faithful to Synge and Lady Gregory, citing them in his Nobel Prize acceptance speech:

When your King gave me medal and diploma, two forms should have stood, one at either side of me, an old woman sinking into the infirmity of age and a young man's ghost. I think when Lady Gregory's name and John Synge's name are spoken by future generations, my name, if remembered, will come up in the talk, and that if my name is spoken first their names will come in their turn because of the years we worked together.

Ever the sense of tradition, the oral recitation of names that the world will not willingly let die. Consciously or unconsciously Yeats harks back to the dawn of Irish literature, the joys of storytelling, the recitation in verse of people and places. He concludes his account with the statement that these two would have been proud to stay beside him on this occasion, "for their work and mine has delighted in history and tradition."

Whatever their degree of friendship, the leading figures had the capacity for sly insult or cutting epigram. The Irish temperament is volatile and swings between sentiment and mockery. Surprisingly enough, it was the mild Æ and not George Moore who defined a literary movement as "five or six people who live in the same town and hate each other cordially." The remark recalls Dr. Samuel Johnson's downright comment, itself Irish in its turn of phrase: "the Irish are a *fair people* . . . they never speak well of one another." This astringent quality keeps the portraits from sentimentality. In the game of verbal give-and-take, the aloof poet Yeats showed a rather unexpected gift. He expressed his resentment of the conservative Professor Dowden of Trinity College, friend of his father's but an opponent of native literature. Dowden, said Yeats, was "a man born to write a life of Southey." The companionable cousins George Moore and Edward Martyn were "inseparable friends bound one to the other by mutual contempt." Moore was notorious for his insinuations about his own wickedness; it was said of him that while a gentleman kisses and doesn't tell, Moore was entirely the opposite. Yeats put it better with his apparently innocuous observation that "I suppose we would both be more popular if I could keep from saying what I think, and Moore from saying what he does not think." As for appearance, Moore was "a man carved out of a turnip, looking out of astonished eyes." It may be that they were astonished at seeing Yeats, who in Moore's phrase, "looked like an umbrella left at a picnic." The unkindest cut was Moore's comment on Douglas Hyde's enthusiasm for Gaelic: when Hyde spoke, the words frothed "like porter" through his moustache, and it was "easy to understand why he desired to change the language of Ireland."

The art of the thumb-nail sketch and the telling anecdote goes back to the eighteenth century. Remarks by Oscar Wilde and his unusual father still circulate in Dublin, such as the observation by Sir William Wilde regarding Professor Tyrrell at Trinity: "If he had known less he would have been a poet." Bulls and epigrams remain in the Dubliner's memory; he is conscious of history as personal history, and the present is always intertwined with the past. Even the eternal subject of Ireland's sufferings was not immune to laughter: "As long as Ireland is silent upon her wrongs, England is deaf to her cries." The popularity of such observations might lead one to conclude that the Irish temperament is incurably superficial, but such is not necessarily the case. Henry Jackson of Cambridge once said of Dr. Mahaffy, the classicist, musician,

churchman, first-rate shot and angler, and master of conversation, that he knew at least three fields well enough
to gain him a European conversation, but his versatility
made him seem superficial. Sir William Rowan Hamilton,
a pioneer in mathematics, became a professor of astronomy
as an undergraduate and was knighted at the age of thirty,
but his real forte was languages, with Latin, Greek, Hebrew, four modern European and five or six Oriental
tongues at his command. When George William Russell
was complimented on his versatility, he used to reply
modestly that a candle does not throw light in only one
direction. Most diverse of all the men of the age of Yeats
was the erstwhile champion cyclist and swimmer, Doctor-
Senator-wit-poet Oliver St. John Gogarty.

Back in the 1790's Sir Jonah Barrington's delightful
skill as a raconteur depended largely upon his art of
characterizing the participants in his anecdotes. One example will suffice. Barrington described Baron Power as
"one of the most curious characters I have met." The
Baron was "a morose, fat fellow, affecting to be genteel,"
and, moreover, was "very learned, very rich, and very
ostentatious." There he stands, the perfect dupe; and after
this opening there will be few to resist the anecdote that
follows. First, the Chancellor's teasing Power because he
in his arrogance could not tolerate the arrogance of the
Baron; next, the gradual effect of a campaign of innuendo,
"first on his pride, then on his mind, and at length on his
intellect." Then the Baron's final "prank," as Barrington
terms it, that of wading into the ocean until he drowned
himself, and the final triumph of the detestable Chancellor, a double victory in that he rid himself of an enemy
and was, moreover, enabled to appoint a submissive suc-

cessor. But our storyteller has not yet concluded, for he remarks wryly that "the precedent was too respectable and inviting not to be followed," and, indeed, to became something of a fashion, in particular by one attorney, who, "for good and sufficient reasons, long appeared rather dissatisfied with himself and other people."

Barrington shows that Dubliners had long been conscious of playing their parts on the relatively small stage of local society. Now with the Irish revival they found themselves playing to a world audience. Their histrionic instincts were quickened, and they seized upon each other as models. Among them none was more popular than Æ. As long as he was around, with his bearded face, mystic gaze, and dreamy soliloquies, it was not necessary to invent the ideal bard. In an early essay, included in *The Celtic Twilight* (1893), Yeats describes him as the "Visionary" who talks "of the making of the earth and the heavens and much else." His poems seem "the very inmost voice of Celtic sadness, and of Celtic longing for infinite things the world has never seen," their melody a "wild music as of winds blowing in the reeds," a phrase Yeats adopted as a title for his verse collection of 1899, *The Wind among the Reeds*. Æ also appears in Stephen Gwynn's novel *The Old Knowledge* (1901), and in George Moore's *Evelyn Innes* (1898) and *Sister Teresa* (1901). His most amusing incarnation is that of the talking philosopher in James Stephens' *The Crock of Gold* (1912). Æ referred genially to several of these portraits, hinting slyly that sales might be improved by his prosecuting the authors for libel. As he neared the age of seventy he still used to enjoy quoting the description of himself in Stephens' *The Charwoman's Daughter* (1912). His casual attire had been hit off exactly: "a tall man with a sweeping brown beard whose heavy overcoat looked as though it had been put on with a shovel." The charwoman's sixteen-year-old daughter, Mary Makebelieve, was curious about him:

> ... he wore spectacles, and his eyes were blue, and always seemed as if they were going to laugh; he, also, looked into the shops as he went along, and he seemed to know everybody. Every few paces people would halt and shake his hand, but these people never spoke, because the big man with the brown beard would instantly burst into a fury of speech which had no intervals; and when there was no one with him at all he would talk to himself. On these occasions he did not see any one, and people had to jump out of his way . . . .

Mary also used to see a young man, thin and black, muttering to himself, "buzzing like a great bee" (perhaps Yeats), and an unkempt man with a pale face and drooping dark moustache (probably Synge), with an odd trick of gazing at one sidewise. Still another, so pale as to look "like the tiredest man in the world" (George Moore), was strangely detached: "He seemed to be always chewing the cud of remembrance, and looked at people as if they reminded him of other people who were dead a long time and whom he thought of but did not regret." But Mary, being her age and being herself, thought more of the massive policeman who directed traffic at the corner of Grafton and Nassau streets, the very corner where Leopold Bloom priced the field glasses in the optician's window and speculated on "parallax," that key word in *Ulysses*, where everything is viewed from several vantage points.

A portrait of Yeats as a young aesthete appears in the description of the composer Ulick Dean in George Moore's

Evelyn Innes. Dean is a tall, thin man with "one of those long Irish faces" and poetic eyes, over which "a heavy lock of black hair was always falling"—the image preserved in the charcoal drawing by Sargent in 1908, or, even better, in the 1900 oil by his father, now in the National Portrait Gallery of Ireland. The novelist points out that his eyes gave the "sombre, ecstatic character to his face"—the dark, deep-set eyes that "seemed to smoulder like fires in caves." Moore has captured the spirit of Yeats in noting Dean's conversations on Irish folklore, and his indifference to men of action: "Shakespeare and Shelley and Blake had never participated in any movement . . . they were the centres of things."

It is interesting that Moore later modified the character to resemble Æ, omitting much of the literary conversation and stressing the bearded and disheveled appearance. Moore added an account of an archeological and spiritual pilgrimage to Tara and Newgrange, a trip which he had taken with Æ and which he describes in *Hail and Farewell.*

Moore's *Ave* (1911), the first volume of his reminiscences, evokes the atmosphere of Dublin in the great days. The time is 1899, and Yeats's *The Countess Cathleen* is about to open, despite protests by the orthodox. Moore has just returned to Ireland, escaping the vulgarity of London, especially intensified by the jingoism aroused by the Boer War. In Dublin, "a town wandering between mountain and sea," the skies are filled with "gentle, encouraging light," and the trim rows of brick houses sun themselves in the May morning. He crosses St. Stephen's Green, impatient with Yeats, who is too preoccupied to look at the children at play or the ducks in the pond. As they go down Grafton Street, Moore observes that Yeats "was willing to talk of Trinity, but not to look at it." They lunch with T. P. Gill, editor of the *Daily Express*, the newspaper which is most receptive to literary news. Only Balzac could have foreseen "the beard, the smile, the courtesy, the flow of affable conversation," but the editor's impractical visions of Irish commercial development exceeded anything in Balzac. That touch of madness must have been invented by Turgenev. Soon we are to meet the handsome T. W. Rolleston, the walrus-headed Douglas Hyde with his drooping moustaches, and the schoolmasterish John Eglinton, and we realize that the three volumes of *Hail and Farewell* are a portrait gallery in prose equaled in humorous observation only by James Joyce's *Ulysses*.

A scene curiously parallel to one in Joyce's *Ulysses* occurs in a literary report contributed by Yeats in 1892 to the Boston *Pilot*. Seated in "the big, florid new National Library," the young poet lamented that all around him were readers "studying the things that are to get them bodily food, but no man among them is searching for the imaginative and spiritual food to be got out of great literature." It is the complaint of young poets everywhere. Would that others were to prove as wrong as Yeats was in this instance! In another ten years this library was to become a meeting place of young Royal University undergraduates, and the scene of one of Joyce's finest chapters, the library episode in *Ulysses*. The spirit of literary Dublin is nowhere better conveyed. The genial Quaker librarian T. W. Lyster still loved and remembered, tiptoes in and out of the office, while the young Stephen Dedalus expatiates on his theory of Shakespeare. Stephen's most formidable opponent is John Eglinton, the library assistant and essayist who later admitted "a twinge of recollection of things actually said." Like a practitioner of the New Criticism, Æ objects to the biographical interpretation, demurring with the remark that "the supreme question about a work of art is out of how deep a life does it spring." When reminded by Frank O'Connor that this quotation is in *Ulysses*, Æ was delighted: "That's very clever of him! . . . I may quite well have said that!" O'Connor drily observes that he said it at least once a day.

The young poet Stephen Dedalus in *Ulysses* bears a mocking resemblance to his creator when he was the insolent Jimmy Joyce in 1904. Stephen's ambitions and attitudes are presented, and, since irony predominates, we see more attitude than ambition. Whatever esoteric significance *Ulysses* has, it tells us much about human nature, particularly in its delightful Dublin form. The book is filled with local tales, for Joyce never needed to invent situations when he could find them in actuality. During the day of the novel we hear about many literary matters, such as the publication of Æ's anthology of *New Songs*, and the new magazine *Dana*, edited by John Eglinton and Fred Ryan. Stephen is rumored to be the only contributor who demands payment; a Joyce poem, "My Love is in a Light Attire," did appear in August, 1904. At the *Freeman's Journal* office, the barrister J. J. O'Molloy remarks to Stephen that "Æ had been telling some yankee interviewer that you came to him in the small hours of the morning to ask him about planes of consciousness." The "yankee" was Professor Cornelius Weygandt, who repeated the tale in his pioneer study *Irish Plays and Playwrights* (1913), without naming the then obscure young man. Weygandt had heard the story from Æ himself and recounted it as an illustration of the poet's influence and his remarkable versatility. On his return home long past midnight, Æ had found a young man waiting in the street outside his house. The elder author had to urge his timid visitor to come in, but even then Joyce hesitated to come to the point. Attempting to put him at ease, Æ asked his guest whether it was economics, or mysticism, or literature that was in question. It was, of course, literature. To his host Joyce seemed "an exquisite," whose opinion was that "the literary movement was becoming vulgarized"—the theme of the essay *The Day of the Rabblement*, about to be printed within a few months. Finally gaining courage, Joyce himself turned questioner, asking whether Æ was "seeking the Absolute." An affirmative reply brought forth a deep sigh from the questioner, who "said decidedly that 'Æ' could not be his Messiah," since "he abhorred the Absolute." Æ sized up his visitor as one of the young men "infected with Pater's relative," and was forthwith relieved to be free of the responsibility. "I wouldn't be his Messiah for a thousand million pounds," he wrote to Sarah Purser; "he would always be criticizing the bad taste of his deity." Professor Weygandt concluded his story with an echo of the departure of the young poet Marchbanks in Shaw's *Candida*: "So the boy—he was not yet twenty-one—went out into the night with, I suppose, another of his idols fallen." But if Æ suggested the self-confident Morrell, the young Joyce, like Marchbanks, had his secret, a secret which commentators have been exploring for almost fifty years, often with frustration, but, more often with delight.

Æ did, nonetheless, recommend his lost disciple to Lady Gregory and to Yeats as "an extremely clever boy who belongs to your clan more than to mine and still more to himself"—an extremely accurate appraisal. Æ thought that

Yeats might find the youth "rather interesting," though he did admit, in another letter, with his characteristically sly humor, "I have suffered from him and I would like you to suffer."

Yeats had never "encountered so much pretension with so little to show for it," yet he too suffered. He was impressed enough to write an account of his interview. Joyce had read several of his own poems, waving aside compliments with the abrupt remark, "I really don't care whether you like what I am doing," and had forthwith raised "objections to everything I had ever done." Yeats made a reply, thinking, "I have conquered him now." But no, for Joyce "merely said, 'Generalizations aren't made by poets; they are made by men of letters.'" As he left, he asked Yeats his age, and, on hearing it, "said with a sigh, 'I thought as much. I have met you too late'"—too late, that was, for Yeats to be influenced by Joyce.

Joyce's remarks to Padraic Colum, later a life-long friend, are in character. In returning an early play, he made the wry comment, "I do not know from which of them you derive the most misunderstanding—Ibsen or Maeterlinck." And Joyce is undoubtedly the person Yeats had in mind in his note to the 1904 edition of *The Tables of the Law*: "I do not think I should have reprinted them had I not met a young man in Ireland the other day, who liked them very much and nothing else that I have written." The diarist Holloway, meeting him at the Cousins' at-home on June 8, 1904, concluded that "He is a strange boy" whom "I cannot forget." Everyone had the same feeling. Professor Weygandt published his anecdote eleven years after he first heard it. The retort to Yeats has a more complicated history. It must have been going the rounds of Dublin, as such remarks will, especially if they are at the expense of Yeats. In 1919, Katherine Hinkson recalled it in her reminiscences, *The Years of the Shadow*, as coming from "an eccentric young Dublin poet who wrote one small volume of exquisite poetry and a book of prose which was banned by the libraries." In later years both participants made attempts to underplay Joyce's asperity. Yeats refers to the remark "you talk like a man of letters" in his *Autobiographies*, and Joyce's *Finnegans Wake* has the buried allusion "I have met with you, bird, too late." The story was printed in Herbert Gorman's first study of Joyce (1924), cut by Joyce from the biography of 1939, and finally restored to its place in literary gossip by Richard Ellmann. It has been asserted, denied, and reasserted; and, amazingly enough, the story remains unchanged in all particulars. In 1907 the popular *Rambles in Eirinn,* by William Bulfin, contained an account of the tourist's meeting a singer at the now-famous Martello Tower, the scene of the first pages of *Ulysses*. This had been only three years before, as were the memories of Holloway and his friend, D. J. O'Donaghue, prompted by Joyce's first book, a volume of poems, *Chamber Music*. He was, they remembered, "a strange boy with wondrous bright eyes," who sat staring at you "until he made you feel quite uncomfortable." His condescension "put you at anything but your ease." One must beware venturing an opinion in his presence, for he "had the art of crushing you with a 'what-do-you-know-about-it-anyway!' sort of sharp remark." Holloway could only conclude: "Ireland has produced some strange people in our time. Few stranger than Joyce!"

Joyce was busy making himself into the image of the artist. He was a good if erratic student, long to be remem-

bered for his wide acquaintance with literature, his unconventional tastes, and his self-assurance. The Royal
University magazine, *St. Stephen's*, has many good-natured
gibes at "Jocax," who, at one meeting of the debating
society, "inveighed with wonted vehemence against his
fellow members for not understanding his sublimities."
He was apparently an unemphatic speaker, delighting in
oblique references to little-known texts. One classmate recalled that he "generally succeeded in mystifying his audience with a heterogeneous jumble of diverse and digres-
sive remarks." He quoted Whitman and Emerson, often
without making his intention clear. Quite in keeping with
his disdain for convention was his losing a chance for a
high rating in a vocal contest because he thought the
sight-singing requirement silly.

Despite the opinion of Yeats, he did have some justifica-
tion for his pretentiousness. At the age of eighteen, only
a second-year man, he had published an essay on Ibsen in
England's leading literary magazine, the *Fortnightly Review*. In the next year he printed, at his own expense, an
attack on the new Irish theatre, giving his opinion that it
was succumbing to "the rabblement." Regarding Yeats,
already famous throughout the English-speaking world:
"It is equally unsafe to say of Mr. Yeats at present that he
has or has not genius." For years he remembered catching
the Dean of Studies on the misuse of an obsolete word in
order to chalk it up to the credit of his hero in his *Portrait
of the Artist*.

His improvidence was as famed as his impertinence.
Dubliners pictured him strolling the streets, and borrow-
ing money by such subterfuges as making change, returning part of the loan on account, and, all in all, engaging in

so many financial manipulations that in the end it was impossible to know who owed whom what.

The talk of the town was that Jimmy was copying down everybody's remarks to include them in a gigantic diatribe against Dublin, a post-Thomist *Summa contra Gentiles*. In *Ulysses*, Buck Mulligan (Gogarty's fictional image) ridicules his friend's expectation of writing something in ten years. As if to answer Gogarty, *Ulysses* is dated 1914–21 on its last page, or ten to seventeen years later. An anticipation of the method of *Ulysses* is found in the remarks of the newspaper editor as he encourages Stephen to write: "Give them something with a bite in it. Put us all into it, damn its soul. Father Son and Holy Ghost and Jakes M'Carthy." Joyce certainly followed the advice. No day has ever been more completely described. *Ulysses* is so permeated with Dublin lore that natives look with a wild surmise at the manic enthusiasm of Americans. It seems unbelievable that strangers could relish the vivid local atmosphere. The characters in the novel traverse much of the city. They chat in pubs, on the streets, and in the library. Gossip occupies their attention, but history is not forgotten. At the newspaper office famous orators are discussed and ridiculed. The editor mentions that the statesmen Henry Grattan and Henry Flood, parliamentary leaders, wrote for the paper shortly after its establishment in 1763; and J. J. O'Molloy quotes admiringly Seymour Bushe's apostrophe to Michelangelo's *Moses* as "one of the most polished periods I think I ever listened to in my life." The arrogant young would-be poet Dedalus, despite his aloofness from the provincial literary scene, is moved, "his blood wooed by grace of language and gesture." The third and climactic instance of oratory in the chapter is

John F. Taylor's famed peroration, comparing the plight of the Irish to that of the Jews in Egypt. Taylor, incidentally, was a formidable antagonist of the young poet Yeats in the National Literary Society, especially in the matter of the selection of titles for the new Irish library, Taylor advocating the staples of old-fashioned rhetoric and propagandist verse, and Yeats opposing him with such fury that, as the poet recalled, "I have known strangers drawn by sport or sympathy to step into the room, and nobody have a mind disengaged enough to keep them out." Taylor may have been jealous of the veteran John O'Leary's interest in the ardent youth, who, on his part, was equally jealous of Taylor's influence on Maud Gonne. In 1904 or 1905 thousands of four-page leaflets defending the Irish language were circulated. Taylor's address was featured, and the title was the orator's final phrase, *The Language of the Outlaw*. Like his creation Dedalus, Joyce himself was so affected by Taylor's bold sweep of language that he chose this passage for his only recording of a portion of *Ulysses*.

Paradoxically, the man who most consistently wrote about Dublin was the one who had most decisively rejected it. Although he was a life-long exile, Joyce often said that in imagination he had never left his native city. Far from accurate, however, are his dramatizations of himself as a solitary genius among Philistines, or his picture of Dublin as a center of "paralysis." Joyce's associates at college were by no means contemptible. They congregated at the meetings of the Literary and Historical Society and at the new National Library. Social evenings were enjoyed at the homes of the young couple James and "Gretta"

88

Cousins, and of David Sheehy, a member of Parliament and the father of a large and lively family. One of the sons, Judge Eugene Sheehy, in his delightful reminiscences, *May It Please the Court* (1951), is probably not exaggerating in considering these college conversations "no mean substitute for the wisdom that emanates from the Professorial Chairs in other Universities." College debates reached "as high a standard during this period as they are ever likely to attain." Judge Sheehy's respect for his friends seems more deserved than Joyce's use of them as uncomprehending foils to his own brilliant Dedalus. Sunday evenings at the Sheehy home were gay with charades and other games. Joyce delighted in doing impersonations and singing comic songs. He admired, shyly, Mary Sheehy, the almost phantom heroine of *A Portrait of the Artist as a Young Man*. Three of the Sheehy sisters married brilliant men—Mary becoming the wife of Tom Kettle, Hannah of Francis Skeffington, and Kathleen of Cruise O'Brien. O'Brien worked with Æ in Sir Horace Plunkett's Irish Agricultural Organization Society. His son Conor Cruise O'Brien has had a distinguished career as historian (*Parnell and his Party* [1957]) and literary critic (*Maria Cross* [1952], a study of modern Roman Catholic writers, published under the pseudonym of "Donat O'Donnell"), as well as becoming one of the best known of modern diplomats, through his service as political adviser to Dag Hammarskjöld and head of the United Nations in Katanga during the Congo crisis beginning in 1960. Kathleen Sheehy O'Brien, an ardent nationalist, may have provided a model for Miss Ivors in Joyce's masterful story *The Dead*. Margaret (another sister) wrote a skit, the performance of which was attended by the indefatigable Joseph Holloway, who found Joyce the only member of the cast who showed any aptitude for the stage.

It must have been a lively group. Judge Sheehy's opinion of the active intellectual life at University College is corroborated by the recently published *Centenary History of the Literary and Historical Society* (1956). Elections were vigorously contested, and programs attracted attention outside the confines of the college. In Joyce's time, inaugural addresses of auditors were on "Realism in Fiction" by Skeffington, later a prominent social critic; "The Celtic Revival" by Kettle, whose career as professor and political leader was, like Skeffington's, to be tragically cut short by violent death; "Irish Genius in English Prose," by Arthur Clery, who attained prominence as a professor of law at the University and as a member of the Supreme Court; and "The Irish University Question," by Hugh Kennedy, who became a member of the Free State's constitutional committee and the first chief justice of the new government. Arthur Clery thought enough of his address to publish it twenty years later in his *Dublin Essays* (1919). Other members of Joyce's college generation to gain distinction in later life were John Marcus O'Sullivan, historian and minister for education; Constantine Curran, recorder of the Supreme Court and expert on Dublin architecture; George Clancy, mayor of Limerick, murdered by the English in 1921; and James Fitzgerald-Kenney, minister for justice. Most dramatic of all were the careers of Thomas Kettle and Francis Skeffington. Although Joyce is far from just to these contemporaries, it is apparent that in spite of being more conventional in outlook, they must have provided whetstones to his mind and constituted a fit audience for his essays on "Drama and Life" (January 20, 1900) and "James Clarence Mangan" (February 2, 1902).

In death as in life Kettle and Skeffington were joined. As college friends, brothers-in-law, fellow workers on *The Nationist* magazine, and members of the Young Ireland Branch of the United Irish League, their careers were parallel. Temperamentally they were opposites. Kettle, genial and witty, a polished speaker, contrasted with his wiry and brusque companion, whose goals were also more extreme. Kettle advocated Home Rule; Skeffington fought for women's rights, joining his wife's name to his, and became identified with the rising labor movement. In college he and Joyce had published at their own expense a small pamphlet, *Two Essays* (1901). These essays, Joyce's attack on the provincialism of the Irish theatre and Skeffington's plea for women's rights, had been rejected by the college magazine, *St. Stephen's.* Those who kept copies have had reason to rejoice in their luck, for not more than eighty-five were issued, and the works of one of the authors have become collector's items. A single copy, in fact, is worth far more than the total printing bill of ten guineas, which, to the printer's amazement, was paid on delivery.

The militant Skeffington pursued a relentless career of reformism. He became a vegetarian, a teetotaler, a non-smoker, and antivivisectionist, like that more famous Dubliner George Bernard Shaw. In his tribute to Kettle the essayist Robert Lynd pointed out the contrast between the two men. While Sheehy-Skeffington marched to meet his aims, Kettle "meditated upon goals." In speaking, Kettle seemed "like the spirit of pity incarnate—some shadow born out of the imagination of Turgenev or Thomas Hardy."

Arthur Clery and Constantine Curran have agreed with Lynd that Kettle was probably the most brilliant man of his generation. His wit was saturnine. An embittered Hamlet, he once defined life as "a cheap table d'hote in a rather dirty restaurant, with Time changing the plates before you have had enough of anything." Although he was a successful member of parliament at Westminster, he had few illusions about politics. His essay on the limitations of political action is a salutary admonition to zealots of every party. "Politics can never be the architect of the New Jerusalem," he warned, "it is not cut out to be much more than a speculative, suburban builder." Even at best, "it will give us a world just good enough to live in." His condemnation of suicide is ironically reversed as a commendation of death, which "has all the attractions of suicide without any of its horrors." His sheaf of essays was appropriately entitled *The Day's Burden* (1910). But he too was capable of humor. He could do a golfing ode to the strains of "The Lost Chord." He could parody Kipling with gusto. He could present the case of Ireland clearly and vigorously. Everything he did—journalism, teaching, politics, writing—he did well. Yet throughout his short career of thirty-six years to everything he seemed to have applied the question which provided the name for a Dublin conversation group, of which Clery and Kettle were members: "*Cui bono?*" "What's the good?" Or, in American, "So what?" An advocate of Home Rule, he feared that whatever program the Liberals supported would be accepted as final. "Life is growth," he said to a large audience on the eve of his election, "growth is change. . . . It may have bivouacs but no barracks." A professor of economics at the university, he defined his subject as "not a science, but a series of controversies with a fixed terminology." Even his patriotism was touched with irony; he modified the epigram about history in applying it to his country: "Irish history is the lie disagreed upon." More bitter is his distinction between the major parties: "When in office, the Liberals forget their principles and the Tories remember their friends." No wonder that Clery said: "You must go to Swift himself, if you would find one to surpass Kettle in that peculiarly Irish quality, sardonic enthusiasm."

World War I divided the sympathies of the two friends. Kettle, in Belgium buying arms for the Irish Volunteers, had been appalled by the German invasion. He cherished the hope that by supporting England during the war Ireland would be rewarded with Home Rule. Sheehy-Skeffington remained pacifist, even disapproving of the aims of the Volunteers as a military organization. Accordingly, Kettle was speaking throughout Ireland in advocacy of enlistment at the same time that his brother-in-law was attacking the war at antirecruiting meetings. Sentenced to six months' imprisonment with hard labor, Sheehy-Skeffington undertook a hunger strike and his sentence was protested in English newspapers by George Bernard Shaw, Robert Lynd, and Conal O'Riordan. On his release, he set out on an American lecture tour in support of Irish freedom, returning to Dublin at the time of the Easter Rising of 1916. He formed a Peace Patrol to prevent looting and violence. Although he was not a belligerent, he was a marked man. Walking home one evening, unarmed and alone, he was arrested, then taken as a hostage on a raiding expedition. Captain Colthurst, in command, shot down an unarmed youth on the road. Sheehy-Skeffington protested this outrage. At the barracks the next morning he was shot without trial, his body buried in quicklime. Subsequently the Captain was court-martialed, found "guilty but insane," and imprisoned for a year, after which he settled in Canada.

Sheehy-Skeffington's death threw Kettle into despair. He rushed into active service. Within three months he was killed. His final resolution, written the day before his death, joins him in spirit with his pacifist-patriot brother-in-law: "If I live, I mean to spend the rest of my life working for perpetual peace. I have seen war and faced artillery and know what an outrage it is against simple men." In St. Stephen's Green, at a place where he used to chat with his students after classes, there stands a bust of this remarkable scholar-patriot. Joyce's Stephen Dedalus had called this park, on which the University College buildings faced, "my green," but it is appropriate to have there a memorial to Kettle, Joyce's constant rival. Kettle's verses, on the pedestal, express his idealism, soaring above the trenches of Flanders:

> So here, while the mad guns curse overhead,
> And tired men sigh with mud for couch and floor,
> Know that we fools, now with the foolish dead,
> Died not for flag, nor king, nor emperor,
> But for a dream, born in a herdsman's shed,
> And for the secret scripture of the poor.

Yeats's constant concern with the heroic personality gave him an Olympian quality, both as man and as poet. Aware from the beginning of his career that he occupied a central place in the revival, he celebrated himself and his friends in verse that is at once a testament of loyalty and an image of nobility for Ireland. Such are the magnificent stanzas of "The Municipal Gallery Revisited," described by him as "a poem about the Ireland we have all served," and the final summation of his philosophy, "Under Ben Bulben." The grandeur of these valedictory poems reveals the poet's sense of drama. The stage itself is always symbolic, whether it be the gracious demesne of Coole Park, the windswept tower of Ballylee, or the sublime silhouette of the mountain Ben Bulben. Before our eyes the present becomes legendary. The poet and his friends share with Timon or with Lear a reality that is beyond mortal experience. Personal vision is transformed into public speech. What is enacted here has universal implications.

Before him always was a heroic ideal for himself and for Ireland, an ideal which was a culmination of the insights of many years. For him nobility involved the stoic virtues of fearless indifference and solitude, combined to create "that quality which is to life what style is to letters—moral radiance, a personal quality of universal meaning in action and in thought." It was this truly aristocratic virtue which he found embodied by Lady Gregory and her estate at Coole. Coole Park became a refuge from the commonness he observed not only on the English throne but among the journalists who attacked Synge and the Dublin politicians who thwarted Hugh Lane in his proposals for a municipal art gallery. In advocating the aristocratic way of life Yeats incurred the risk of snobbery, the idolatry of a hollow shell taken as a reality. Art is aristocratic, for the poet, as Aristotle noted long ago, seeks examples among princes. Not that these figures are of greater spiritual worth, but because they, by their exalted status, enlarge and lend grandeur to the moral condition of experience.

Yeats's views of personality developed in a time of bitterness. The years between 1907 and 1912 marked the end of his hopes for practical success in the theatre and in Irish politics. He was entering middle age, and few of his friends were untouched by the passage of time. His ideal was based on the insights of years, including the examples of his friends O'Leary and Synge, and the views of his father. Blake and Shelley and Nietzsche merely revealed to him what he was already discovering in himself, and in an Ireland freed of the sentimentalities of the Celtic Twilight or the simplifications of the patriot.

Theories about the value of personality and its cultivation had constantly preoccupied the poet's father. Few better spokesmen could be imagined. John Butler Yeats was apparently a lovable person. Æ recalled his "enchanting flow of conversation" and noted that all his portraits "seem touched with affection." The artist's impromptu sketches of his son as well as those of most of the figures in the revival are well known. The reason for their charm, Æ continued in his introduction to John Butler Yeats's *Essays, Irish and American* (1918), is that "nature's best gift" to the painter was "a humanity which delights in the humanity of others." Joined with these engaging traits was an incurable habit of theorizing. For years he spun out his notions about the artistic personality, relating it to the love of life and the play of imagination, tracing its effects on national temperaments, and urging its nurture through education. These theories were expounded in essays and lectures, but chiefly in letters to his son. At times it must have been somewhat tedious and overwhelming. One may smile at this father of a great poet pushing definitions of poetry at his son and requesting comment, while the forty-

or fifty-year-old Yeats apologized for not complying, often excusing himself because a typist had not yet transcribed the minute scrawl. Yet the elder Yeats was apparently a most disarming egotist. Even though he never ceased to recount with pride his successes as essayist or dinner-table conversationalist, he admitted that "not only am I an old man in a hurry, but all my life I have fancied myself just on the verge of discovering the *primum mobile.*"

Whatever friction there may once have been between them, it was gradually replaced by mutual respect and love. It must have been something of a comfort to Yeats to have his dominating parent separated from him by the Atlantic Ocean when John Butler Yeats settled in New York City in 1908. The letters of father and son make fascinating reading, as they engage in a spirited give-and-take over the issues of art and life. In 1910, Yeats acknowledged his surprise at discovering how much of his own outlook had been inherited, and two years later he suggested to his father "a great project" of an autobiography. Unfortunately only the brief *Early Memories* was completed, to be published in 1923, a year after the father's death.

What wisdom lies behind J. B.'s aphorisms! "Poetry concerns itself with the creation of Paradises," he wrote, and "working and caring for children makes one anxious and careful of them, but amusing them makes one fond of them." Like the silvery sound of laughter, the genial philosopher's remarks on personality run through his correspondence. A constant contrast is that between will and imagination. The man of action lives in an atmosphere of opinion and morality, seeking to praise or denounce, to devour life rather than to enjoy it.

The beginnings of the poet's meditations on personal-

ity are to be found in the essays published as *Discoveries*
(1907). "We must ascend out of common interests," he
urged, "but only so far as we can carry the normal, passionate, reasoning self, the personality as a whole." In
another essay, its title taken from John Donne, *The Thinking of the Body*, he urges that "art bids us touch and
taste and hear and see the world." Thus the Victory of
Samothrace "reminds the soles of our feet of swiftness,"
and, in contrast to a lifeless Canaletto, a Venetian view
by Francken makes one "long to plunge into the green
depth." Fifteen years later Yeats reverted to another more
extended pictorial contrast. In *The Trembling of the Veil*
(1922) he compares Strozzi's portrait of a Venetian gentleman (a Hugh Lane gift to the Dublin National Portrait
Gallery) to Sargent's portrait of President Woodrow Wilson. In the former, "whatever thought broods in the dark
eyes" seems to have "drawn its life from his whole body."
Should the thought change, so would the pose, "for his
whole body thinks." Wilson's eyes alone are intent; all else
—face, hands, clothing—inert, reflecting the modern loss
of Unity of Being.

The diary of 1909, portions of which were issued as
Estrangement and *The Death of Synge*, and later incor-
porated into the *Autobiographies*, reflects the poet's concern with personality. Style in literature, manners in life
provide "the only escape from the hot-faced bargainers."
Both are possible through discipline, which, deliberately
created, assumes a pose, disinterested enough for charm,
committed enough for passion. In contrast to passive obedi-
ence, active virtue is "theatrical, consciously dramatic, the
wearing of a mask." Of these values Synge is chosen as
exemplar. Fearless of his impending death, unmoved by

criticism, completely absorbed in his vision of existence, Synge was above opinion and above detraction. In their isolation "from all contagious opinions of poorer minds," Synge and Lady Gregory were "the strongest souls I have ever known." In his Nobel Prize speech he cited their work for Ireland, conscious, he said, "of how deep down we have gone, below all that is individual, modern and restless, seeking foundations for an Ireland that can only come into existence in a Europe that is still but a dream."

Yeats's autobiographical volumes, beginning with the *Reveries over Childhood and Youth* (1915), are as rich in characters as in theories of character. The portraits of Oscar Wilde, William Morris, and John O'Leary are memorable; those of Madame Blavatsky and George Moore memorable and malicious. Throughout his recollections he emphasizes the need for some simplifying and unifying image, and searches for links with men of preceding ages, concepts which were playing an increasing role in his poetry.

The first fruit of these concerns was the magnificent elegy on Robert Gregory, who had been shot down over Italy in 1918. Lady Gregory's son, artist and sportsman, remains a shadowy figure. It is just as well. Biographical fact should pale in the blazing light of this apotheosis. His death was the kind of grand gesture beloved by the romantic imagination. His military service itself set him apart, for the war was unpopular in Ireland, and futile as far as Irish national aims were concerned. Yet this life of varied promise, tragic in its brevity, became a symbol of fulfillment. Like the ideal Renaissance courtier, Gregory had attained, if only for an instant, true Unity of Being. The moment of glory was but a brief flare, like a comet in the skies, as he met his death in the purer elements of fire and air. His death also presaged the end of the aristocratic Anglo-Irish tradition, and the end of an Ireland that Yeats had learned to respect. In keeping with the dignity of the theme the verse movement is stately and traditional, with Spenserian echoes. Deceptively casual in tone, it breaks off with the ultimate silence of one striken by grief. The poem embodies one of the most ancient of literary forms, a roll call of the noble dead.

Two thousand years ago a notable Roman wrote that great men had lived before Agamemnon, but, lacking poets to celebrate them, they are forgotten. In recalling those names immortalized by Yeats, the words of Horace come to mind. John O'Leary, too proud to complain of mistreatment in prison, too noble to stoop for patriotic ends; John Synge, and the cousins John Shawe-Taylor and Hugh Lane; and the marked man of the Free State Government, Kevin O'Higgins, "the finest intellect in Irish public life," Yeats called him; and, foremost of all, that second Helen of Troy, Maud Gonne—to recite this list is to call up the heroic age of Ireland.

IV - Politics

THE scientific efficiency of modern warfare no longer permits man to die with dignity. War has left the plane of human tragedy to become mass slaughter, beyond comprehension and almost beyond pity. During the Irish wars of independence personal heroism was still possible. Although Dublin remained virtually under seige from 1916 to 1923, the conflict was largely a contest of individuals. Men had some freedom to choose their fates. They could fight for ideals and attempt deeds of daring. They were led by poets and commemorated by poets. It was a literary war, and if the paradox be permitted, it might be called the last human war.

Most of the leaders had the Irish instinct for self-dramatization and were capable of the grand gesture. Michael Collins, a price on his head, became a legend in his own lifetime. Almost singlehandedly he managed the war in his multiple roles of minister of finance, director of intelligence, director of organization, and adjutant general.

For three years he outwitted pursuers, and he is still remembered for such exploits as cycling unarmed past military cordons, or chatting unconcernedly with the detectives sent to track him. Dying in the Easter rebellion, The O'Rahilly wrote his signature on the pavement with his own blood. Six years later the insurgent commander Cathal Brugha, trapped in a burning building, rushed into the street to confront his attackers, blazing revolver in his hand as he fell.

Brugha's dying act seems to typify the prevalent sense of fatality. The 1916 patriots calmly regarded their revolt as a blood sacrifice. Two leaders of the Free State had premonitions of their doom. In signing the Treaty in 1921, Collins felt that he was signing his death warrant. Within a year he was killed. His successor, Kevin O'Higgins, said that "No man can expect to live long who has done what I have done." Winston Churchill, though an implacable opponent, characterized O'Higgins as "a figure from the antique cast in bronze." In the unhappy duty of establishing order in the new Free State, O'Higgins had been forced to the desperate expedient of executing prisoners as a deterrent to the lawlessness of the country. Among the victims was his old friend, comrade, and best man at his wedding, Rory O'Connor. Another was the stubbornly Republican leader Erskine Childers, who had broken with his fellow patriots on the issue of the Treaty. Executed for illegal possession of firearms, Childers was carrying a revolver given him by Collins, once his friend and so recently his enemy. During ensuing raids the father of O'Higgins was murdered, and, at last, in 1927 he himself met the fate he expected, being shot down on a Dublin Street. As he died in agony he said, "I forgive my murderers." His friend Yeats, hearing of this tragedy, walked alone for hours, inconsolable.

The stern necessities of such a time might be expected to preclude any literary expression, but this was not the case. As the "great man in his pride," O'Higgins is the unnamed hero of Yeats's eloquent poem "Death." Yeats also celebrated The O'Rahilly, and his lines on the Easter Rising are among the triumphs of his art. The early plays of Sean O'Casey and the fiction of Liam O'Flaherty and Frank O'Connor depict these sordid and stirring times. The Irish struggle for independence was tragic in the truest sense of the word, for heroes were to some degree responsible for their fates, and they were great men who suffered greatly.

History was also to blame; political pressures, mounting for generations, rose to explosive violence and more than once threatened to destroy the very nation they were creating. Independence was finally won for part of the country but at a sorry cost. If something less than philosopher-kings, the leaders of the Irish Republic were unquestionably dedicated idealists and commanding personalities. The Easter Rising of 1916 was manned and led by poets. And few of the principals survived the tragic drama.

To understand the complexities of the story, some background is required, yet it is worth the effort, for the motives were admirable. Mr. Conor Cruise O'Brien, editor of the useful lectures by Irish historians on *The Shaping of Modern Ireland* (1960), remarks that "confusion is the condition in which history exists." In Ireland this confusion was further confounded by divided allegiances and frustrations caused by alien domination. In this picture, roads seem to point in all directions, or in none. Parliamentary agitation, passive resistance, and outright rebellion were advocated. The goals were equally varied, from complete independence to Home Rule. Leagues, clubs, and societies proliferated, their programs sometimes complementary, more often contradictory. Irish nationalism was fed by many streams.

As a young man, tired of the aestheticism of London, Yeats plunged into politics with an unthinking zest which was amplified by his admiration for the unbelievably beautiful and unattainable Maud Gonne. Intoxicated by the only popular success he ever achieved, he made speeches, wrote letters to newspapers, and toured rural Ireland, finding himself everywhere the center of applause. He later reflected in his autobiography that "It was many years before I understood that I had surrendered myself to the chief temptation of the artist, creation without toil." His political activity culminated in the presidency of a committee to arrange celebration of the centenary of the 1798 uprising. He had hoped to reconcile factions. Again, he made a bitter self-judgment: "It was no business of mine, and that was precisely why I could not keep out of it." In addition to the influence of Maud Gonne, there was the noble figure of John O'Leary, veteran of five years in prison and fifteen of enforced exile, a man whose vision was large enough to accept the poetic achievements of the Unionist Sir Samuel Ferguson, and even to forgive those who had imprisoned him: "I was in the hands of my enemy, why should I complain." Some of the most eloquent pages of Yeats's autobiography are devoted to this figure whose patriotism was second only to his integrity. The young disciple was often to remember his remark that "There are things a man must not do to save a Nation."

Throughout his life Yeats regarded O'Leary as the ideal Irish patriot.

The agitations of these years flash through the autobiography with kaleidoscopic brilliance and brevity—a meeting organized by the laborer James Connolly, later to be executed in the 1916 Rising; gatherings of Italian and French sympathizers; crowds smashing windows. It was a tumultuous time, and far removed from occult or poetic pursuits. Then Yeats dropped politics. Estrangement from Maud Gonne was a factor, as well as the new-found patronage and hospitality of Lady Gregory, and his interest in establishing an Irish theatre. In her memoirs, *A Servant of the Queen,* (1938) Maud Gonne MacBride watches with amusement the rivalry between the two supporters of the theatre—Miss Horniman with the money, Lady Gregory with the brains. Yeats could not fail to contrast the generous enthusiasm of his patrons with the bigotry of patriotic clubs.

The domination of England falls like a shadow across Irish history. Dublin had been a bridgehead for invaders since the time of the Danes, and the English early consolidated their foothold within the Pale of the country. Crushing wars of extermination under Queen Elizabeth and Cromwell were followed by penal laws. The effect of these drastic restrictions on freedom in religion, language, education, and property was well described by a lord chancellor who summed up the legal status of the Irish Catholic: "The law does not suppose any such person to exist." So appalling was the tale of massacre and devastation that Irish history has been called something "for Englishmen to remember, for Irishmen to forget." It is difficult, indeed, to see the other side of this question. One can scarcely overestimate the hatred which had been built up over many generations in a people who saw their lands ravaged and expropriated, their cities sacked, and their monasteries and churches profaned and destroyed. Ireland still bears the scars. In almost every town weeds and wild flowers grow within the roofless walls of battered cottages. Not far away there may stand in solitude a gaunt stone keep or a ruined abbey.

The Irish problem has been said to rest in the fact that the English have for centuries tried to rule a people brighter than themselves. However that may be, the heartening fact is that the race continued to exist. Accustomed to living by their wits, the Irish have often conquered their conquerors in the same way. Ireland has not only survived; it has retained much of its inheritance. It has even assimilated its enemies. *"Hibernis ipsis Hiberniores"* was long ago said of those, "more Irish than the Irish," who succumbed, notably the Norman settlers who were not only to provide leadership during the ensuing centuries but to become the staunchest champions of the natives. Such supposedly Irish names as Fitzgerald, Butler, Desmond, and Burke come from these Danish and Norman families.

In the time of Yeats one finds every shade of allegiance from the imperial scarlet of the Dublin Castle "garrison" and their supporters, the Unionists, often sneeringly termed "West Britons," to the defiant orange of Protestant Ulster. Various hues of native green might represent the degrees of Home Rule or Republican sentiment. At the farthest extreme is the blue of O'Duffy's short-lived Fascist movement and the Communist red of O'Casey. It might be supposed that the Anglican ascendancy would support their status, but from this very class came Lady Gregory and Maud Gonne. Synge's family, also from this background, never saw one of his plays on the stage, and, had they thought of the matter, might have been a little confused by the fact that his Irish dramas were being hissed by Catholic Nationalists while audiences were kept in some slight semblance of order by the hated police.

Glorious as the ideals of Irish patriots sound, they were often conflicting, even mutually exclusive. Their partial fulfillment or failure reveals the fanatic blindness or inexperience of their advocates. Political and religious zeal do not breed tolerance, and there are often heartbreaking consequences. The moderate are forced to stand aside, helpless at their inability to control the flood of passion. One thinks of the gentle scholar Eoin MacNeill, head of the Irish Volunteers, not consulted in plans for the Easter Rising. Pearse's words to him echo the tragic tensions of these times: "Yes, you were deceived, but it was necessary."

The story of the Irish fight for independence is not simply a heroic melodrama. We encounter the anguish of suffering and the pathos of defeated hope. There are tragic ironies too, and even roguish humor, for the clever Irishman often wins over superior forces by his own ingenuity. One instance was the case of defying the English prohibition of all public meetings except those held for recruiting. Nationalists scheduled so many patriotic meetings on the same day that it would have required a gigantic police force to break them up. As for the recruiting meetings sponsored by the English government, with embarrassing frequency there happened to appear on the platforms eloquent Sinn Fein speakers.

Often bravery became mere bravado, for the fatal fascination of rebellion easily induced a romantic urge to die as a martyr rather than live as a slave in an insufferable environment. With the authority of personal experience Sean O'Faolain, in his study of *The Irish* (1947), has classified the rebels as one of the country's five basic types, the others being the peasantry, the Anglo-Irish, the priests, and the writers. In O'Faolain's analysis, the rebel displays a devotion to failure, a heedless immaturity, for, lacking any tradition of statesmanship, his is the simple belief that "Death did not mean failure so long as the Spirit of the Revolt lived." Certainly the tradition of rebellion has long been cherished. Its emotional force has proven to be irresistible. Each generation has contributed its quota to the roll of martyrs, and each has been aware of its predecessors. Harry Boland recalled this tradition in speaking during the Treaty debates of December, 1921. Friend of the two antagonists, Michael Collins, "The Big Fellow," and Eamon de Valera, "The Long Fellow," Boland, himself fated to die in the forthcoming Civil War, cited the words of Pearse, the hero of the Easter Rising. Pearse had traced the proud lineage back to the seventeenth century, in which "the veterans of Kinsale fought at Benburb, the veterans of Benburb fought with Sarsfield at Limerick." From the risings of 1798, Pearse said, an unbroken sequence led to 1916: "The man who defended Emmet lived to be a Young Irelander; three veterans of the Young Ireland Movement then founded Fenianism; and the veterans of the Fenian Movement stood with the Volunteers of 1916." In no other country do speeches of defiant idealism play so large a part in the national heritage, whether in Parliament, from the prisoner's dock, or from the scaffold; and legend and ballad quickly follow events in this haven of the oral tradition. Theobald Wolfe Tone and Lord Edward Fitzgerald head the list, and give it an aristocratic air. Their participation in the Rebellion of 1798, together with the belated protest of Robert Emmet in 1803, was the fountainhead of popular patriotic poetry, namely the stirring lines of John Kells Ingram, "Who fears to speak of Ninety-Eight?" and Emmet's final statement at the gallows: "When my country takes her place among the nations of the earth, then, and not till then, let my epitaph be written." Thomas Moore, a friend of Emmet's, contributed to the legend with the elegy for Emmet's fiancée Sarah Curran, who died of a broken heart after marrying an officer and going with him to Sicily: "She is far from the land where her young hero sleeps." Other popular songs give romantic versions of the Rising of 1798. The pathetic ballad of "The Croppy Boy," trapped in 1798 by an officer impersonating a priest at the confessional, and the stirring "Boys of Wexford" commemorate the occupation of that southern town by a band of insurgents, armed only with pikes.

Much of this verse has the immortality of subject matter and memorable rhetoric rather than that of profound insight. Often it is merely the politics of black and white, expressed in Moore's "Song of O'Ruark":

> *On our side is Virtue and Erin!*
> *On theirs is the Saxon and Guilt.*

Yet it must be admitted that the association of Saxon and guilt is one of long standing in Ireland. The earliest of English totalitarian wars against an entire population was that of Queen Elizabeth's commander Lord Mountjoy. His "scorched earth" policy had appalling effects which left an indelible impression on the loyal civil servant Edmund Spenser. Although Spenser, like Swift, was an unhappy exile, disappointed like Swift in his failure to gain promotion, and although he wrote his *View of the Present State of Ireland* (1596) as a bid for advancement, he could not conceal his horror at the devastation in Ireland: "Out of every corner of the woods and glens they came creeping forth upon their hands, for the legs could not bear them; they looked like anatomies of death, they spake like ghosts."

Less sensitive than Spenser, the lawyer-poet Sir John Davies applauded himself for his establishment of the plantation system, the settlement of English exploiters (rightly termed "undertakers") on lands confiscated from their Irish owners. To the Attorney General this system of organized robbery could be regarded as "the masterpiece, the most excellent work of reformation," in which glorious activity and natives were, "with sword, pestilence and famine," prepared to become proper "admirers of the Crowne of England." Yet it was soon necessary for Cromwell to subdue ruthlessly these "admirers of the Crowne." In Irish matters, it seems, the English lose all sense of irony. After putting to the sword the entire population of Drogheda, Cromwell exulted that "It has pleased God to bless our endeavours."

No policy of persecution could exterminate Irish loyalty. The pride in an ancient civilization gives a manly tone to the laments of the last bards, a note that Yeats cherished in his late poems. In one magnificent elegy Egan O'Rahilly (1670–1726) voiced his own farewell to life and art as well as the death of a tradition:

*I will follow the beloved among heroes to the grave,
Those princes under whom were my ancestors before the
death of Christ.*

Yeats, who advised Frank O'Connor in preparing this
translation, echoed the theme in "The Curse of Cromwell"; even though lovers and dancers "are beaten into
the clay," the old man retains his pride as a servant:

His fathers served their fathers before Christ was crucified.

From the time of Cromwell to that of the Easter Rising
of 1916 the Irish suffered a series of defeats. The famed
line from James Macpherson's *Ossian*, "They came forth
to battle, but they always fell," might seem the epigraph
for the race. There was the rout of James II at the Battle
of the Boyne (1690), followed by the exploitation of the
Irish which infuriated Jonathan Swift a generation later.
The eighteenth century ended with the disastrous rising of
1798, and the shameful closing of the Irish Parliament in
1800 by an Act of Union, passed by open-faced bribery of
the deputies. The nineteenth century saw a tiresome repetition of crushed hopes and broken lives. In 1829, Daniel
O'Connell, "The Liberator," secured the emancipation of
Catholics by refusing the test oath on his election to Parliament, yet he, at the height of his power, dispersed a monster audience of thousands who were ready to assert their
rights. This aborted meeting at Clontarf in 1843 led to his
being prosecuted for conspiracy. Although the verdict was
reversed, his health and influence declined. The next in
the succession of disasters was the blight that destroyed
the potato crops of 1845 and 1846. It has been said that

there was enough grain in Ireland to keep the population alive, but landlords demanded their rents, with the sickening result that steamers loaded with grain and cattle were being shipped to England while almost one million natives died, often to the accompaniment of the battering ram on their cottage walls. It was, the London *Times* admitted, "a real, though artificial, famine." Hundreds of thousands fled in ill-kept emigrant "coffin ships." Without exaggeration, Lord John Russell could declare to the House of Lords in 1846; "We have made Ireland . . . the most degraded and most miserable country in the world."

Incitements such as these could scarcely be without effect. A steady pressure for reform, often interrupted by violence and illuminated by heroism, continued throughout the century. The Young Ireland party centered around *The Nation*, which published the popular verse of Thomas Davis and other romantic nationalists. This unsophisticated poetry, like that of Tom Moore a few years earlier, gave to the world the sentimental picture of Ireland which stood in the way of Yeats, Synge, and Joyce. The now forgotten William Rooney (1873–1902) was the last of these newspaper "bards," and his posthumous *Poems and Ballads* was hailed by Arthur Griffith, who had joined Rooney in founding the influential weekly *The United Irishman*. Clearly Rooney was a man to be respected by patriots. One can imagine the antagonism aroused among such patriots by the review of the young James Joyce, just graduated from college, who found the poet "almost a master in that 'style' which is neither good nor bad." The verse was described as "a false and mean expression of a false and mean idea," in that the author had been diverted from literature to patriotism. Even though his work might "enkindle the young men of Ireland to hope and activity," as Rooney's admirers claimed, art, continued the reviewer, "is a stern judge." Yet "he might have written well if he had not suffered from one of those big words which make us so unhappy"—a phrase which Joyce remembered for fifteen years, when he put it into the mouth of Stephen Dedalus in the second chapter of *Ulysses*.

More violent tactics had been advocated by the "Physical Force" wing of the Young Ireland group, led by John Mitchel whose *The United Irishman* had openly advocated rebellion. (This revolutionary weekly, founded in 1848, had ceased publication and given its title to the Griffith-Rooney journal.) It was the year of revolution in Europe, and the fervor swept up even the moderate aristocrat William Smith O'Brien, of the ancient line of the Earls of Thomond, a family descended from Brian Boru. O'Brien, whose former conservatism had provoked the quip that he was "too much of a Smith and not enough of an O'Brien," was captured in a skirmish. He was found guilty of treason, but the sentence of death was commuted to transportation for life, and after eight years in Tasmania he was allowed to return home. John Mitchel's *Jail Journal* (1854) is a patriotic classic. The policy of violence was carried on by two groups founded in 1858, the Irish Republican Brotherhood and the conspiratorial Fenians, named for the ancient warriors of Ireland. The cloak-and-dagger atmosphere of Irish political action was established, with raids and assassinations countered by the activities of spies and paid informers, always under the threat of imprisonment, transportation, or execution.

One of the last Fenians was the venerable O'Leary, to whom Yeats could always turn when disheartened by the pettiness around him. Yeats's political disillusionment had begun amidst the quarrels of political clubs in the 1890's, and was intensified by the shock of Maud Gonne's marriage to the adventurer John MacBride, from whom she shortly separated. On an American speaking tour at the time, Yeats was stunned by the telegram which brought news of the marriage. Years of haggling with those who attacked the theatre, and contempt for the niggardly attitude of Dubliners toward supporting a Municipal Art Gallery, led Yeats to pen those lines of the poem "September, 1913," in which O'Leary in the grave became a symbol of the death of romantic Ireland. So it might have seemed when in 1913 a paralyzing lockout of 24,000 laborers was bringing suffering and violence to Dublin. But Yeats disregarded the problems involved in the gallery dispute— choice of site, design—and, even more, was unaware of one of the most romantic actions in Irish history, the forthcoming Rising of 1916.

Constitutional reform had reached its greatest power under the leadership of Charles Stewart Parnell in the 1880's. This haughty man, who could confront incrimination with an icy stare, appealed to the Irish imagination. Yet his position was made precarious by allegations of conspiracy based on evidence which, it turned out, had been forged by a common adventurer. Vindicated by a commission of inquiry, he returned to take his seat in the House of Commons amid the thunderous applause of his fellow members, most of them his opponents. Parnell walked down the aisle without making any acknowledgment, as indifferent to acclaim as he had been to denigration. It was an episode that appealed to the equally proud James Joyce. Joyce recounted it in one of a series of articles he wrote for the Trieste newspaper on the subject of Irish politics.

But Parnell could not survive a marital scandal. His love for the married Kitty O'Shea had long been a matter of common knowledge, but the granting of a divorce in November, 1890, brought about a debacle. The Irish Parliamentary party wavered; Gladstone and Cardinal Manning brought pressure. At a caucus in a committee room of the House of Commons, Parnell was deprived of his party leadership, only twenty-six of the seventy-one fellow members staying helplessly with him. He took his case to the country, but he and his new wife Kitty were showered with abuse, and once lime was thrown in his face. Less than a year later he was dead. The nine-year-old James Joyce never forget his hearing the news at boarding school, nor the painful family quarrel at the Christmas dinner table, one of the most effective scenes in his *Portrait of the Artist*. The painter Jack Butler Yeats used to recall seeing Joyce's father at a Parnellite rally. It must have been the great gathering in the Rotunda, outside of which now stands the plinth to the memory of Ireland's "Chief," as he had once been admiringly called. In her intimate biography Mrs. Parnell quotes Katherine Tynan Hinkson's description of the torchlight parade, the roaring crowd, and his hour-long speech, "simple, direct, suave—with no device and no artificiality," yet, undramatic as it was, "listened to with intense interest, punctuated by fierce cries against men whom this crisis had made odious, now and then marked in a pause by a deep-drawn moan of delight."

Dead, Parnell immediately passed into legend. It was symbolic of the conflict between love and politics in the youthful experience of Yeats that the poet, meeting Maud

Gonne at the port of Kingstown (Dun Laoghaire), found himself submerged in the crowd awaiting the return to Ireland of Parnell's body. Thousands paid their final tribute, and as the coffin was lowered into the grave a meteor streaked across the sky. The romantic national historian Standish O'Grady was reminded of similar portents associated with the death of St. Columba.

The boy Joyce wrote a verse elegy, which his proud father put into print and distributed to friends. The poem is lost; one speculates over how many rounds might be provided for the spirits of John Joyce and his thirsty and impecunious friends if a copy were to turn up at auction today.

Joyce's brother Stanislaus recalled a few lines only, but it may be a memory of this childish poetic effort that finds utterance in the banal verses recited by Mr. Hynes in the *Dubliners* story *Ivy Day in the Committee Room*. And is not the shabby canvassers' quarters, the scene of this story, an ironic reminder of that notorious committee room in the House of Commons where Parnell's career was doomed, and Ireland's fate was decreed? Parnell was to Joyce a symbol of the ideal Ireland, and his betrayal became a paramount factor in Joyce's hatred for whatever was cowardly and shoddy in his native land. The sense of betrayal was a traumatic experience for the Irish people at large, in that they were finally forced to face the fact that the national problem was not simply one of domination from outside. Most extreme of all, Joyce's Stephen Dedalus abjured all allegiances—to pope, king, or country.

In the case of Arthur Griffith we see a companion tragedy to that of Parnell. Parnell failed grandly, but Griffith failed by succeeding. His truculent attacks on English rule inflamed his countrymen to go beyond his own halfway stage of independence, and he died with his country in civil war, torn by the forces he had set loose. In 1899, having returned from two years in South Africa, he established the nationalist weekly *The United Irishman*. A printer's apprentice, self-educated, he carried on a campaign for the separation of Ireland from England. His solution was that Ireland should have a semi-independent status like that of Hungary, and his editorials on the subject appeared in book form in 1904 under the title *The Resurrection of Hungary*. Ireland must have her own parliament, develop her own industries, renew her own culture. A stout fighter and an uncompromising publicist, Griffith gained strength from his very limitations. He despised clerics for their rejection of Parnell, hated the labor leader James Larkin, and was blind to the art of Yeats and Synge, finding them anti-Irish. He scorned "any such myths as English justice or English mercy." From Mary Butler he took the name "Sinn Fein," Gaelic for "we ourselves," the title of a ballad of John O'Hagan. In 1905 a conference elected him chairman of the movement; a daily paper, *Sinn Fein*, was established in 1906. It was the height of the party's control of nationalism. But soon the tide was to flow past Griffith's mild notions of a dual monarchy. The old Fenian Tom Clarke, veteran of fifteen years in prison, was reviving the Irish Republican Brotherhood and preparing the Rising of 1916, because of which he, at the age of sixty-eight, was to be the oldest victim of the English firing squad.

With so many divided counsels it is amazing that the Rising ever took place. Another 1916 leader, James Connolly, had been calling for armed insurrection. While the secret military tribunal of the I.R.B. was laying plans, Connolly's labor paper *The Worker's Republic* asked, in an editorial of January, 1916, "Are we not waiting too long?" Clearly something had to be done by the I.R.B., but just what was done is still a matter of dispute. Was Connolly kidnapped by the I.R.B. leaders, as has often been asserted, when he disappeared for three days in January? Or did he go willingly to a prearranged meeting? The answer is buried in conjecture. Nevertheless, some agreement must have been made, for the small Citizen Army was induced to delay their uprising until the agreed date of Easter week. Even so, the orders were twice rescinded, and only a portion of the expected force participated.

Connolly had gained his leadership of labor during the bitter six-month lockout of 1913–14 by the Dublin Employers' Federation. Severe hardships had been suffered, but the cause of labor won the support of Yeats, James Stephens, Seumas O'Sullivan, Æ, and many other cultural leaders. As Connolly said, "the working-class has lost none of its aggressiveness, none of its confidence, none of its hope." Most effective of all statements supporting labor was Æ's trenchant open letter "To the Masters of Dublin," published in *The Irish Times*, October 7, 1913, accusing the employers of insolence and ignorance and concluding with a warning that they were "blind Samsons pulling down the pillars of the social order."

The most important legacy of the long strike was the militant though inadequately trained Citizen Army. Its history was first written in 1919 by an obscure Dublin laborer Sean O'Cathasaigh, later known as Sean O'Casey. The fifteen pounds he was paid by the Dublin publisher for *The Story of the Irish Citizen Army* was the first he earned by his pen, but most of it went to pay for his mother's funeral. His frenzied efforts to cash the check make one of the pathetic episodes in his autobiography.

Meanwhile other troops were drilling, much to the amusement of the Dublin passers-by, who laughed at the oddly clad groups holding Sunday and holiday drills, and even pretending to attack Dublin Castle. One month after the formation of the Citizen Army the Irish Volunteers had been organized, under the leadership of the Gaelic scholar Eoin MacNeill. In the Northern Protestant counties the Ulster Volunteers had been drilling for over a year, with the connivance of the government. Thus there could be no objection to the appearance of these uniformed groups, wearing slouch hats and bandoleers, and often carrying only wooden guns. In addition to the three unofficial armies, the English stationed some ten thousand soldiers in Ireland, and about the same number of armed police, the Royal Irish Constabulary. The Irish Boy Scouts (Fianna Éireann) and the League of Women (Cumann na mBan) were also active. Well might the schoolmaster-patriot Padraic Pearse say to a Brooklyn audience early in 1914: "There is again in Ireland the murmur of a marching."

Every chapter of the story passed quickly into verse. It was thoroughly in keeping with the spirit of these times that Ernie O'Malley concluded many episodes of his classic autobiography with popular ballads. In quality this poetry ranges from mere sentimental jingles to the magnificent verse of Yeats.

In an effort to provide arms for the Volunteers, guns were smuggled into Dublin in July, 1914. Surprisingly enough, this violation of a government order had a Junior

League coloring, with the suggestion arising from Mary Spring-Rice, daughter of Lord Monteagle and cousin of the British Ambassador in Washington, Sir Cecil Spring-Rice. It was planned at the London home of Mrs. Alice Stopford Green, who like her late husband J. R. Green was known as an historian. The journalists Darrell Figgis and Erskine Childers were in the group, as well as Sir Roger Casement, knighted for his salutary work in the Congo.

The arms were landed at the port of Howth from three yachts, with Miss Spring-Rice and Mrs. Childers among the crews. When news of the event reached the Castle, a detachment of Scottish troops was sent to block the approach to Dublin. In the city some shots were fired, killing three of the jeering crowd and wounding others. The victims were accorded military funerals, and their names were acclaimed, while the troops became popularly known as the "King's Own Scottish Murderers":

> *On Bachelor's Walk a scene took place*
> *Which I'm sure had just been planned;*
> *For the cowardly Scottish Borderers turned*
> *And fired without command . . . .*

A surer poetic touch is found in the verses commemorating the capture and execution of Sir Roger Casement. The stark simplicity of the lines recalls that of time-honored English and Scottish ballads. In Germany, Casement had arranged for the smuggling of arms to Irish patriots. At the last moment, realizing that the scheme could not succeed, he came to Ireland in a German submarine to attempt the cancellation of the plans. It was just before the celebrated Easter Monday of 1916:

> *'Twas on Good Friday morning all in the month of May*

A German ship was signalling beyond there in the Bay;
"We've 20,000 rifles here all ready for to land,"
But no answering signal came to them from lonely Ban-
    na Strand.

There follow the scuttling of the German ship, Casement's
capture, and his pathetic end:

'Twas in an English prison that they led him to his
    death,
"I'm dying for my country," he said with his last breath,
He's buried in a prison yard far from his native land,
The wild waves sing his Requiem on the lonely Banna
    Strand.

The Easter Rising of 1916 is closer to the Irish heart
than similar memories—Verdun or Valley Forge—to other
peoples'. The name itself conveys a religious aura, appropriate to the miracle of freedom born of martyrdom.
To be sure, its harvest was belated and the sacrifice was
not understood at the time. Again Yeats became the voice
of Ireland. His surprise, and even annoyance, were those
of the country, as was his later reverent awe. No one has
questioned the dedication of the leaders. Failure was almost inevitable, with its penalty of death. At his court-
martial the scholarly leader Padraic Pearse expressed the
spirit of the patriots: "We seem to have lost, we have not
lost . . . we have kept faith with the past, and handed a
tradition to the future." It was a remarkable group. All
that we learn of them testifies to their idealism and nobility. Thomas Clarke was the first signer of the proclamation of independence by virtue of age, but Padraic Pearse
was deservedly president of the Republic. Hitherto he had
not been unusually prominent, and James Stephens did

not expect that one with so little personal magnetism would become the leader. Yet Pearse was a man of considerable depth. As he awaited execution he wrote the inexpressibly moving verses of "The beauty of this world has made me sad," which Yeats considered one of the finest poems of modern Ireland. Pearse, imbued with the national spirit, onetime editor of the Gaelic League journal, founder of Irish schools for boys and for girls, had been preparing himself and his students for the sacrifice. In his book *The Pope's Green Island* (1912), W. P. Ryan had devoted a chapter to him as "The Hero in the College," who was "the most courageous pioneer" in Irish education. Characterizing Pearse as "a scholar with a child-spirit, a mystical temperament, and a Celtic nature," Ryan pointed out his consistent efforts "to inspire his pupils with a love for the high heroic ideals of Gaeldom." His farewell to the school at the beginning of the Easter recess is deservedly remembered. It was, like most of his utterances, a reminder that each generation must testify to its allegiance, regardless of cost. A striking figure, tall and handsome, he was also inclined to intervals of quiet meditation. His full force was apparent only on the platform, one of his most famous speeches being that at the burial of Jeremiah O'Donovan Rossa, an old Fenian, in 1915. In his peroration he taunted the English and prophesied Ireland's liberation: "They think that they have foreseen everything, provided against everything; but the fools, the fools, the fools!—they have left us our Fenian dead, and while Ireland holds these graves Ireland unfree shall never be at peace."

Like Pearse in his activities as poet and translator was the young lecturer in literature at University College,

Thomas MacDonagh, who also taught at Pearse's schools. In contrast to Pearse, he seems to have been a jovial companion, with a feeling for the humor of native life. He was also the most considerable scholar among the leaders of the I.R.B., his study of Irish literature showing a sensitive knowledge and taste. With the invalid poet Joseph Plunkett, MacDonagh had helped found the nationalist Irish Theatre and edit *The Irish Review*. Two other editors were among the victims, James Connolly of *The Worker's Republic* and Séan MacDiarmada of *Irish Freedom*.

The action was brief. On Monday, Dubliners paid little attention to the ragged groups of militia with their makeshift equipment—nothing unusual, really; indeed so familiar a sight as not to seem ridiculous any more. Then the news broke. One group had taken the General Post Office, raised a tri-colored flag (a legacy from Young Ireland days of 1848); and Pearse had read the proclamation, beginning with the words now so deeply burned into Irish hearts:

> IRISHMEN AND IRISHWOMEN: In the name of God and of the dead generations from which she receives her old tradition of nationhood, Ireland, through us, summons her children to her flag and strikes for her freedom . . . .

South of the river the Citizen Army was in St. Stephen's Green, and scattered points were being held throughout the city by the Volunteers, most noteworthy being Boland's Mills, where a young mathematics teacher, de Valera, was guarding the approach to Dublin from the port of Kingstown. British forces quickly fought their way into the city; a gunboat shelled Sackville Street. The seige could not be long, for soon the Post Office headquarters were ablaze. By

Sunday evening Dublin was quiet, broken. The story of this week has been retold again and again, but seldom better than by James Stephens. *The Insurrection in Dublin* (1916) reveals the surprise, confusion, and heroism of the week.

The protracted executions during the month of May turned the sympathies of bewildered citizens to the cause. The most controversial figure was Sir Roger Casement, captured on the west coast and brought to London for trial. A man of commanding presence, he won the sympathies of many English people, and a defense fund was raised. Henry Nevinson, Robert Lynd, and George Bernard Shaw were among those concerned about the case. The irony of being prosecuted by F. E. Smith, now attorney general, who had once defied the law in respect to the Ulster Volunteers, was not lost on Casement. In his magnificent final speech the accused referred to "Unionist champions" who "chose a path they felt would lead to the woolsack, while I went a road I knew must lead to the dock." As for the charge of treason: "Judicial assassination to-day is reserved only for one race of the King's subjects, for Irishmen . . . . In Ireland alone in this twentieth century is loyalty held to be a crime." Even the staid London *Times* could grant that he won the attention of the court as "he seemed to seek for remembrance among that band of dreamers and patriot threnodists who have figured so conspicuously in the recent misfortunes of Ireland."

Casement's character is still debatable. No final decision has been reached regarding the insinuations of perversity, so unbelievable in a man of his character. The suspicions were based on notorious "black diaries," the authenticity of which has been questioned, especially in view of Casement's exemplary record in exposing atrocities in the Congo and in South America. Then, too, Irish minds have not forgotten the Pigott forgeries about Parnell. The diary material was not used in the trial, as it was obviously irrelevant, but it was circulated among English and American officials to deflect outrage against the hanging and to prevent Casement's becoming a martyr. These tactics failed, and Yeats poured out his scorn upon those who "turned a trick by forgery" in order to blacken "his good name." A good name, indeed, had been his. Stephen Gwynn thought him "one of the most noble creatures I have known." He had won the respect and friendship of Joseph Conrad, Conan Doyle, and many others.

Another patriot whom Yeats commemorated in his verse, lamenting her transformation from her carefree girlhood, was Constance Gore-Booth. From an old Sligo family, she was the most unlikely of revolutionaries. Raised amid a society of hunts and balls, she studied painting in Paris, where she married a fellow artist, Count Markievicz. On their return to Dublin, they became active in the theatre. The Countess next turned to the nationalist cause. In 1909 she urged that instead of establishing Boy Scout groups, Ireland should organize patriotic units. Many agreed, although no one seemed willing to accept responsibility. She did not hesitate, for, as Æ said, "she was a fine, breathless character . . . devoid of fear." The consequences of her interests were surprising. Her fine home was often watched by detectives; artists and writers mingled there with laborers and social celebrities, while on her well-tended lawns young boys might be practicing rifle drills. In the Dublin lockout of 1913 her militant energy found a practical outlet in food kitchens and clothing depots. A leader in the 1916 Rising, she held the College of Surgeons for five days and was one of the last to surrender. She was at first sentenced to death, then to life imprisonment, then released, and was often imprisoned again. In 1918 she became the first woman to win election to a national parliament, and, together with her fellow Sinn Fein delegates, met in Dublin on January 21, 1919, to proclaim the Irish Republic. In the debates on the Treaty she, an uncompromising Republican, joined the other women closely associated with the rising—Mrs. Pearse, mother of two victims, Mrs. Thomas Clarke, and Mary MacSwiney, sister of the hunger-striker—to vote against its acceptance.

In view of its impact on Irish history, the rising was comparatively small. Of course two orders for its cancellation had been issued, and the response from the areas outside Dublin was meager. Twenty years later an Irish Roll of Honor listed 1,528 participants, some 200 of whom were of the Citizen Army. Losses numbered about 450, civilians and combatants, to the English loss of 130 out of approximately 2,000. Of the outcome there was never really any doubt, except to one imprisoned Volunteer who replied to Prime Minister Asquith that he thought it was a success. Asquith was incredulous, and asked how such a conclusion was possible. The prisoner replied, "Well, if not, what are you here for?"

The cause was lost, for the time being. In general, Dubliners had not approved of the rising. Many Irishmen had enlisted in the English Army, and their dependents, known as "separation women" because of their government allowances, often hissed nationalists as slackers. Of course the English had not made very convincing pleas for enlistment when they urged the Irish to fight for the freedom of other small nations. The culminating irony was the English praise of Belgium for providing the Irish with schools, for it was the English Penal Laws which forced Irish Catholics to go abroad for their education.

James Stephens concluded his eyewitness account with the prophecy that, though the country was not yet sympathetic, "in a few weeks she will be, and her heart, which was withering, will be warmed by the knowledge that men have thought her worth dying for." The executions of the leaders, sickeningly spaced over a period of ten days, soon changed the mood of the country. Douglas Goldring, the English novelist, arrived one month later to find Dubliners already revering the victims, standing thoughtfully before their pictures in the shop windows. Stephens confessed to Goldring that he was ashamed of not being among the fighters. He should, he thought, have been in one of the three places, "in my grave, in jail, or on the roofs." Goldring's book *Dublin Explorations and Reflections* (1917), by "An Englishman," is a valuable firsthand report not only of the city just after the Easter Rising but of its intellectual and social life at a time when most of the literary lions were on show.

The commemoration of the Easter martyrs by Yeats in his "Easter, 1916" is one of his most powerful utterances, gaining additional force from the fact that the poet is honest enough to express his own surprise, and doubt, about the action. The casual acquaintances he had unthinkingly accepted, and derided, have been transfigured by self-sacrifice. Rumor had it that at first Yeats was annoyed that he had not been consulted, and for years he had protested against the narrowness of politics. Now he makes handsome amends, and pays tribute to the heroism which had been so unexpected—yes, even from the "inglorious lout" MacBride, who had married Maud Gonne.

Two companion poems by Yeats develop further implications. "Sixteen Dead Men" contrasts the futility of logic and argument when the heroic dead, silent though they be, continue to dominate the consciousness; "The Rose Tree," in ballad manner, attributes to the idealistic poet-educator Pearse the sentiment that the "right Rose Tree" of Ireland can be nourished only with "our own red blood."

Meanwhile the tragicomedy of English mismanagement dragged on. The government was fated to reap the harvest of past bad faith, since its intentions were always suspect. A garrison of forty thousand troops was needed to police Ireland, at the very time when the army was suffering drastic losses in the Somme offensive. Lloyd George's government wavered between severity and leniency. Political prisoners were deported without trial. Then, without warning, they were released, arrested again, released, and rearrested. It was embarrassing to have Irish elections for Parliament being won by patriots interned in English jails, and still more baffling to find that the Sinn Fein victors—there were four in 1917—were holding true to Griffith's principles in refusing to sit at Westminster. Faced with the necessity of replacing the men killed in Flanders, England contemplated conscription for Ireland. The Irish, having no voice in national affairs, resented this threat of compulsion in a war that was not their own, feeling that military service would compromise the nationalistic cause.

One final attempt was made to solve the Irish question. In June, 1917, Lloyd George summoned a Convention

to formulate Irish policy. It included representatives of
county and municipal governments, churchmen, spokesmen of labor and of chambers of commerce, and appointees
of each of the political parties, including Sinn Fein. Sinn
Fein and the All-for-Ireland League refused to attend. The
final membership of ninety-five, although hand-picked, did
include such eminent liberals as the reforming landowner
Lord Dunraven, the parliamentarians Stephen Gwynn
and John Redmond, Æ, and his employer, Sir Horace
Plunkett, who was appointed chairman. But the sessions
were secret, and soon it became apparent that the delibera-
tions were to be controlled by the Cabinet. The result was
that several members resigned, among them Æ, and finally
in April, 1918, the Convention adjourned without recom-
mendations. In striking contrast, a brief conference at the
Mansion House in Dublin, attended by members of the
Parliamentary party, the Irish Trades Union Congress,
Sinn Fein, and the All-for-Ireland League, quickly agreed
that "the passing of the Conscription Bill by the British
House of Commons must be regarded as a declaration of
war on the Irish nation," a position supported by a statement of the Roman Catholic hierarchy.

With conflict unavoidable, it is just as well that the
Armistice came before any attempt was made to introduce
conscription, because Irishmen were perfecting their own
homemade weapons. The collapse of the Convention, the
rising power of Sinn Fein, and the death of John Redmond
in March, 1918, spelled the end of parliamentary methods
regarding Ireland. The election of December, 1918, was
clearly a mandate for an Irish Republic (the meaning was
apparent even after the censor had cut most of the words
in the Sinn Fein manifesto. The results exceeded all ex-

pectations. Sinn Fein made an almost complete sweep of what is now the Republic of Ireland, all of their sixty-nine candidates winning. Twelve of these had been under sentence of death, and twenty-one others had been condemned to imprisonment. On January 21, 1919, the first session of the Dail Eireann, the Irish Parliament, opened in Dublin. It proceeded to elect de Valera president, even though he was still imprisoned in England. In orderly fashion governmental departments were established, and a hearing at the Paris Peace Conference of 1919 was requested. President Wilson answered an Irish delegation in words that reveal his dilemma in being unable to activate his own visions of freedom for minorities:

> You have touched on the great metaphysical tragedy of today. When I gave utterance to those words I said them without the knowledge that nationalities existed which are coming to us day after day.

The lurid light of violence throughout six tragic years makes the historian's task impossible. Impartiality is unattainable, and often even simple accuracy, too. Outrage engendered further outrage. Ambush was met with reprisal. Armed bands, some official, others mere lawbreakers, raided banks in search of funds, assaulted and murdered suspicious persons, took army barracks to gain weapons. The English garrison had no enemy to attack, and their own methods were the shabby forms of suppression—raids, arrests, reprisals. Novel types of military sadism developed—the search of hospitals for wounded fighters, the carrying of hostages in lorries to deter ambushes. Erskine Childers, the English publicist who became a leader of the Irish Republicans, described Dublin in the days of the terror:

As the citizens go to bed, the barracks spring to life. Lorries, tanks, and armoured searchlight cars, muster in fleets. . . . and, when the midnight curfew order has emptied the streets—pitch dark streets—the weird cavalcades issue forth to the attack.

It is the world of Liam O'Flaherty's *The Informer*, of O'Casey's *Juno and the Paycock*, and many short stories and melodramas.

In March, 1920, the police force was increased by English auxiliaries, former officers of the army, and the dreaded "Black and Tans," so called from their mixed police and army uniforms, black trousers and boots with khaki coats. This undisciplined band of vagrants carried on a campaign of casual frightfulness which is still remembered even in recent days of organized terror. Their aimless machine-gunning of civilians, burning and sacking of towns, and other barbarities were excused and even encouraged by a Divisional Commissioner of the Royal Irish Constabulary who was reported to have addressed the men in June: "Sinn Fein has had all the sport up to the present, and we are going to have the sport now." As for the murder of civilians, "You may make mistakes occasionally and innocent persons may be shot, but that cannot be helped, and you are bound to get the right parties some time." With such statements and actions becoming known, civilized public opinion was outraged.

The dashing Michael Collins led the Irish to victory by an expertly co-ordinated counterespionage system whose information was speedily transformed into action by the strikes of his "flying columns" of raiders. It was a cloak-and-dagger war, although it often came down to sordid murder in back streets and boarding houses. Collins outwitted all the spies sent to trap him, and his experiences form a saga. His explanation of his almost miraculous survival was simple: "I do not allow myself to feel that I am on the run," a state of mind which "prevents me from acting in a manner likely to arouse suspicion."

An Irish correspondent for the London *Globe* expressed his amazement that "every step taken by the Castle is known an hour afterwards," which is uncanny enough "to make sane men believe in spirits." Collins had contact with spies in government offices, of course, and the feats of intercepting mail, of detecting forgeries, and of tracking secret agents are still recounted. One time, it was said, he was pinned down by a detective who gloated in his catch, whereupon Collins quietly suggested that there were people about. Along the street and in doorways were men in trench coats, lounging and watching, hands in pockets. The detective walked away.

As important as the gathering of information was the dissemination of news and propaganda. The fascinating tale of Irish political periodicals awaits adequate treatment. No one has screened the numerous editorials written by Arthur Griffith over a period of twenty years to demonstrate his power as an almost Swiftian satirist. One of his journals, in answer to British censorship during the European war, was a compilation of accidentally relevant quotations on the subjects of freedom and nationality. Griffith could not be accused of writing the passages from the Constitution of Norway, the patriotic poets, or old newspapers! Appropriately entitled *Scissors and Paste*, it was issued for only three months during the winter of 1914–15, but its psychological value was incalculable. Another of Griffith's journals, *Nationality*, is an example of the editor's mastery of the weapon of irony. He defines the post of Lord Chancellor by pointing out that his salary would buy a bottle of stout for every minute of his life and still leave thirty shillings a day in his purse. He usually stays in office only about four years, then "he retires to make room for another Lord Chancellor." His strenuous efforts are repaid by a pension of four thousand pounds, providing he does nothing. The final descriptive tag brings home the marriage of politics and economics: "He is devoted to the Empire."

In *Four Glorious Years* (1953), David Hogan has recounted the vicissitudes of the *Irish Bulletin*, issued from November 11, 1919, to December 13, 1921, without interruption, despite constant raids and even the theft of the mimeographing machinery. Ingeniously disguised as an insurance society, the office was on the floor above a crown solicitor's. At one time English detectives conducted a house-to-house search, but they never thought of looking above the crown solicitor's rooms! Another time the printing machinery was seized and the Castle issued some forged releases of invented Sinn Fein "propaganda," a move that was immediately discovered. The climax of this exposure of England's "government by forgery" came with the detection that an official Castle typewriter had been used to fabricate threatening letters, which, typed on stolen Dail Eireann stationery, had been created to show that Sinn Fein was, as Lloyd George was calling it, a "murder gang."

A saga was beginning to surround Eamon de Valera, the "convict 95" of the popular ballad:

'Twas in Kilmainham prison yard our fifteen martyrs died

*And cold and still in Arbour Hill they are lying side by
side,
But we will yet pay back the debt for the spirit is still
alive
In men who stood through fire and blood with convict
95.*

Another song of the time concluded with the line, "And
we'll crown de Valera King of Ireland!" No other Irish
leader has undergone so many jail experiences. His death
sentence having been commuted to life imprisonment after
the execution of the other leaders, he was released in June,
1917, as part of Lloyd George's attempt to appease the
Irish—with a Convention meeting on Home Rule it was a
little ironical to have the universally acclaimed head of the
Irish independence movement in prison.

Less than one year later he was again arrested, together
with other leaders, for participation in a presumed conspiracy with Germany. His subsequent release from Lincoln Jail belongs to romantic fiction rather than to reality.
A fellow prisoner had sent out a postcard with comic cartoons labeled "Christmas, 1917" and "Christmas, 1918."
The first depicted an intoxicated householder fumbling
with his key and muttering, "I can't get in." The second
showed a prisoner with a key, saying, "I can't get out." But
the key was an exact drawing of the prison chaplain's, made
from an impression in wax taken from the chapel candles.
The recipient was more perceptive than the unsuspecting
censor of the mail, and shortly an accurate facsimile was
smuggled into the prison. With this duplicate de Valera
unlocked the gate on the night of February 3, 1919, to
meet Michael Collins and Harry Boland, his rescuers.

As violence reached a climax, moderates on both sides

expressed alarm. Arthur Griffith, interned in England, made the accurate prediction that "if this sort of thing goes on, we will end up by shooting one another." Such was soon to be the fate of both Collins and Boland; on opposite sides of the Civil War, each was shot in ambush. English authorities faced impossible decisions. Their enemy was all about them, in civilian clothes. It was an undeclared war, with no clearly designated leadership. Edgar Holt, in his history *Protest in Arms* (1960), illustrates the confusion by recounting a conversation of the time at the palace of the Archbishop of York. The four men present, all churchmen, took four different views of the Irish problem—complete support of English authority, hesitant acquiescence in establishing order, full sympathy with the Irish, and a suggestion that the question be referred to the League of Nations.

For the most part, English policy might be fairly described by the then popular phrase, "cruelty well applied." Prisoners were tortured for information; they were forced to join "identification parades" in which they filed past barriers which hid unknown observers straining their eyes to recognize wanted men. The hunger strike became a formidable weapon of resistance. Sixty men refused food for ten days in Dublin's Mountjoy Prison. Outside, crowds kept a constant vigil in the streets, praying, singing patriotic songs, and shouting encouragement. In retaliation the authorities invoked what was known as the "Cat and Mouse" act, releasing the weakened prisoners and rearresting them when they had regained their strength. Both hunger-strike and "Cat and Mouse" tactics had been used in the suffragette agitations in England, but they became internationally known from their application in Ireland, especially after the incredibly long hunger strike of Terence MacSwiney, lord mayor of Cork, ended with his death on the seventy-fourth day, October 25, 1920.

Two weeks later Lloyd George prematurely exulted at a London banquet, "we have murder by the throat." But even as he spoke Michael Collins was tracking down army intelligence officers in Dublin in preparation for the coup of "Bloody Sunday," November 21, when fourteen suspects were assassinated in their homes. Martial law was invoked, but ambushes continued. In the face of anarchy the old excuse of maintaining law and order was wearing thin. English and American public opinion were pressing for an end to the terror. Negotiations were undertaken, but meanwhile the English government in Ireland was effectively paralyzed by the destruction of the Customs House, with its file of civil records. Finally a truce became effective in July, 1921. The Commander in Chief of the English forces in Ireland, General Sir Nevil Macready, exclaimed that nowhere but in Ireland could one find at the same time "open rebellion, martial law, peace proposals and a general election."

Yet the truce was only a brief intermission. For five months Irish and English delegates consulted, until Lloyd George used the requisite combination of canniness and charm to threaten war if the Irish delegates refused to sign the Treaty in December, 1921. It is clear that among the Irish leaders de Valera was the only match for Lloyd George. In his exchanges of the late summer with the English Prime Minister he always had the upper hand, with his "attitude of extreme reasonableness, and his air of injured innocence," to quote his biographer Denis Gwynn. In every case he pierced through the Prime Minister's verbiage, noting that "it is idle to say that such a conference would be 'without prejudice,' " and that "it is precisely because neither side accepts the position of the other that there is a dispute." But de Valera had refused to go to London, sending instead a five-man delegation of moderates with uncertain instructions.

It was truly a "Peace by Ordeal," to use the title of Frank Pakenham's classic study of the Treaty. Under pressure, the delegates capitulated without communicating with Dublin. Ireland was to remain under the crown, with a possibility of partition. No independent republic had come into being.

In Dublin, de Valera was about to preside at a Dante centenary celebration in the Mansion House. He was putting on his academic robe when Eamon Duggan arrived from London with the news that the Treaty had been signed and was to be released to the press in a few minutes. De Valera received the news in bitter silence. In the words of M. J. McManus, the scholarly President of the lost republic "sat there, stonily impassive, his heart like a stone, in profile bearing a striking resemblance to the great Florentine whose memory was being honored."

The aftermath was heartbreaking. The lengthy Treaty debates convey the anxiety of the time. Did acceptance imply defeat, or was it a necessary compromise on the way to freedom? Was further resistance possible? "I see no alternative"—"I did not forget these things and yet I signed"—"We lost the Republic of Ireland in order to save the people of Ireland"—"It is an outrage on the memory of our martyred comrades." Arthur Griffith pleaded that the Treaty "has no more finality than that we are the final generation of Irishmen." De Valera rose to make a final appeal: "We have had the record of four glorious years, years of magnificent discipline . . . . The world is looking on at us now . . . ." But he was unable to finish. The Treaty was accepted by a vote of 64–57, and the assembly broke into tears, the spectre of civil war before them, the sad burden of failure behind.

To ardent Republicans, "perfidious" England had once more turned the trick, transforming an Irish victory into a surrender. The result seemed national suicide, a slave state rather than a Free State, the terms dictated rather than ratified democratically. De Valera noted that Griffith was left in the position of maintaining the Republic with one hand and knocking it down with the other. Republican feeling was summarized in the words of Liam Lynch, chief of staff of the Irregulars: "We have declared for an Irish Republic and will not live under any other law." In all fairness to the English delegates, it must be noted that two conservative leaders, Sir Austen Chamberlain and Lord Birkenhead, sacrificed their political futures by being a party to the Treaty.

What we now know of personal jealousies among the Irish leaders throws some light on the tragic anticlimax of Irish hopes in the Treaty of 1921, and the disastrous Civil War that followed. Today the bitterness of this dissension seems far greater than the traditional hatred of England. A Dubliner put the matter wittily: "Our history ends in 1921; after that we have nothing but politics." Experts have reached no agreement on the matter, partly because of a lack of evidence but more because in the very inquiry one must begin with the acceptance of a political bias.

It is impossible to attempt here any solution of a problem that has worried Irishmen for more than forty years, but the basic questions may be outlined. First, what authority did the five Irish delegates have to empower them to sign the Treaty? Considerable ambiguity exists; they were termed "plenipotentiary," yet instructed to submit the Treaty to the Irish Cabinet before acceptance. An almost final draft was nearly accepted by the Cabinet three days before the final signing. Michael Collins had written in a letter to a friend a month before, "From Dublin I don't know whether we're being instructed or confused. The latter I would say." Secondly, what more could the delegation have hoped to get? Two undesirable features might have been modified: the Oath of Allegiance to the Crown, and the acceptance of the separation of Northern Ireland. However, the Ulster leaders had opposed a united Ireland since Home Rule had first been broached in the 1880's. Finally, once the treaty had been signed, what could the Irish government do about it? The country could not stand another war, as the destruction of the next few years was to prove. Moreover, England had placed herself in the position of making a reasonable grant to Ireland— something less than complete freedom, to be sure, but enough to cast the burden of proof on Ireland for refusing it.

Kevin O'Higgins once remarked that 20 per cent of the opposition to the Treaty was idealism, 20 per cent crime, and the rest sheer futility. In retrospect, several "might-have-beens" can be spotted. Had the first Declaration of Independence (January 21, 1919) been less specific, it would not have been interpreted as an outright mandate for a republic, a mandate violated by the Treaty. Had the army been more clearly under the authority of the Dail during the war, the possibility of its revolt would have been lessened. Had anti-English propaganda not been so violent, settlement with England might have seemed less humiliating, and aspersions of treachery not so readily forthcoming. Had the Treaty not been signed so precipitately, it would have been accepted in better faith, and, had it been submitted to Cabinet or Dail, the onus would not have fallen on the delegates.

Without any such moderating circumstances, confusion was inevitable. Personalities seem to have been a disrupting factor, in the Dail and among the delegates. Between the moderate position of Griffith and the irreconcilable attitude of Brugha stood Collins and de Valera. Public support had not been consolidated behind any single policy or any single leader. The army was a potential source of disruption, since guerrilla fighters followed local leaders, and the methods of combat favored individual deeds of daring rather than co-ordinated efforts.

As in the most poignant dilemmas, no one was really to blame. Political inexperience may have caused the delegates to accept continued allegiance to the crown and the division of the island; at least there is a suspicion that Lloyd George and Winston Churchill were bluffing in their threats of war. Although the delegation could not have been expected to guess this, it does vindicate de Valera in his insistence upon a unified, independent Ireland. The unbearable stresses of the time may excuse the failure of pacts, conferences, and elections in ensuing months; yet the final cease-fire left the country more ravaged than ever. Ironically enough, time and peaceful means were finally to gain independence, if not the end of partition. And, by another of the many ironies of Irish history, independence, when it came, was won by de Valera through taking advantage of the achievements of his chief rival. In 1931, Cosgrave, successor of Griffith and Collins, had been president of the government when the English Parliament proposed what was to be known as the "Statute of Westminster" which guaranteed the status of Commonwealth members as "autonomous communities freely associated," the definition adopted by the Imperial Conference of 1926.

After the high idealism of the struggle for freedom, the Civil War was a sorry anticlimax. Undoubtedly there was still idealism on both sides, but violence proved unavoidable. Former companions fought savagely, and to the outside world it seemed as though the fair name of Ireland was being besmirched by the Irish themselves. When it came to guerrilla warfare, there was little to distinguish Free Stater or Republican from Black and Tan. The war in Europe had halted emigration, and hordes of young men constituted a threat to order. In addition, mere boys had taken to arms. In rural districts it was easy for the unscrupulous to indulge in theft and arson, and with combatants in civilian clothes, war sometimes of necessity became indistinguishable from murder.

In its sad efforts to enforce order among its own people, the government was forced to adopt the hated methods, and even the arms, of the English. Imprisonment without trial, the taking of hostages, the execution of prisoners in retaliation, the use of spies and informers—all the sordid yet dramatic means of warfare were practiced. Again Yeats immortalized the time as the "blood-dimmed tide" of that magnificent poetic evocation of historical crisis, "The Second Coming." In the "dragon-ridden" days of 1919 he had prayed that his daughter be spared. He had refused to

celebrate the Allied side in the war of 1914–18, but the
Irish wars threw deep shadows on his poetry. To his
friend Sir Herbert Grierson, editor of Donne, Yeats expressed his horror at the outrages. Since none seem immune to the frenzy of blood, "we may learn charity after
mutual contempt."

The breakdown was catastrophic, and even now it is impossible to assign responsibility or to ascertain motives.
Hesitant to invoke military action, the Provisional government permitted the disaffected army leaders to hold the
Four Courts building as their headquarters, yet for the
forthcoming election of June, 1922, the government failed
to correct the election rolls, and it produced the new constitution so late—the very morning of the balloting—that
few could study it. Collins had also entered into a pact
with de Valera, only to be rejected at the last minute—a
plan for a coalition slate which would at least have stalled
the crisis. Meanwhile the recently retired Chief of Staff,
Field Marshal Sir Henry Wilson, military adviser for
Northern Ireland and recently elected member of Parliament, was making inflammatory anti-Irish speeches in
the House of Commons at the very time when Collins and
Griffith were in the visitors' gallery. Within a week of the
election, Wilson was assassinated in London. The English
were about to return to police Ireland when the Provisional government attacked the Four Courts. A bitter
parody of Robert Southey's famous poem on the Battle
of Blenheim later appeared in the Republican newssheet
The Fenian, on October 3, 1922:

.   .   .   .

It was the English gave the shells
That tore the Four Courts down;

It was for Ireland's good, they said;
  For Ireland and the Crown.
'Tis English shells, you know, must be
  At every famous victory.

. . . .

The General Post Office had been gutted in 1916; the classic Customs House had been fired in 1921 to paralyze English legal administration. Now the third, and most beautiful Dublin landmark was destroyed, as were large areas in the center of the city. For many years these monuments stood as gaping ruins, grim reminders of the pall of sorrow that hung over the country.

The cost in leadership was even greater. Brugha died rather than surrender to his former friends. De Valera's associate Harry Boland was killed in a raid on his quarters. In August, 1922, the two leaders of the Free State government perished within ten days of each other, Arthur Griffith collapsing and Michael Collins dying in an ambush near Cork. Erskine Childers, whose connection with Irish independence had continued from the time of the Howth gunrunning in 1914, and who had served as secretary to the Treaty delegation, was captured and executed for illegal possession of weapons. In answer to complaints in the Dail about the severity and brutality of law enforcement, Kevin O'Higgins, minister for home affairs, admitted that "executions are terrible, but the murder of a nation is more terrible." Earlier Arthur Griffith had sadly refused the plea of his friend Maud Gonne MacBride for leniency toward prisoners with the words: "We are now a government; we have to keep order."

The Republican cause died in a holocaust. In November, 1922, the Speaker of the Dail received a letter from the "Chief of Staff (for Army Council)" of the Irish Republican Army threatening all members who had voted to military courts the power to inflict the death penalty. Shortly thereafter two deputies were fired on in the street, one fatally. In reprisal, four imprisoned Republicans, among them the leaders Liam Mellowes and Rory O'Connor, were executed without trial, and before the end more than seventy followed. Meanwhile railroads, factories, and public buildings were being destroyed. In January a policy of attacking the personal property of government supporters was inaugurated. The houses of the Earl of Mayo and of Sir Horace Plunkett were burned, the latter with a fine collection of books and pictures. Senator Oliver St. John Gogarty made his celebrated escape from kidnapers, but his house in Connemara was burned. Free State officials were forced to remain in hiding, and often lived for days in the government buildings. During the next few months many more fine homes were destroyed, including Moore Hall, the County Mayo house of George Moore's brother Maurice. Fortunately the terror was of short duration. The army was pushed into the hills and thousands were imprisoned. At last a cease-fire was proclaimed in May, 1923. De Valera lamented "the ever rising tide of bitterness" and "the vanishing of the common dream of national regeneration." Alas, every word is true. But how, historians are still led to ask, how could it have been prevented?

Under these conditions, to serve in the government demanded sheer physical courage. Members had to meet secretly, and to live under close guard. A grim reminder of the time is to be found in the neglected fantasy by Æ, *The Interpreters* (1922), a platonic dialogue taking place in a prison of a beleagured city. Each of the spokesmen—poet, capitalist, labor leader—attempts to define the manner in which a nation may be fulfilled. A later, more pessimistic version of his speculations on *The National Being* (1916), *The Interpreters* leaves one with the same feeling as do so many of his other works—it is so fine that one wonders why it isn't better.

Æ was suggested for the Senate, but he refused. In the circumstances he was probably wiser than Yeats, who saw the causes he espoused invariably meet with defeat. Yeats failed in his major effort, his defense of the right of divorce, although no one can deny that his remarks on the subject (in the debate of June 11, 1925) were tactless and offensive, vaunting as he did the superiority of the Protestant Irish tradition and pointing to the domestic morality of three prominent heroes, the "Three Statues" of the epigrammatic poem, Parnell, Nelson, and O'Connell. His two most important committee projects, the Irish Manuscript Commission and a Federation of the Arts, were shelved. He was unable to regain the Hugh Lane pictures. His six-year Senate term expired before the act to establish censorship came up for debate in 1929. He made known his position, and, had he served a second term, he would again have been defeated. The older he grew, the more unruly he became. Swift was in his mind, as well as the aristocratic thinkers of the eighteenth century. He showed interest in a semi-Fascist group, the Blueshirts, and wrote for them marching songs which cannot be sung and cannot be marched to. He played the irresponsible beggar, delighting in improprieties, hinting that church and state are the mob howling at the door. Even though he could write in the *Spectator* in 1932 that "there have been few mistakes," and that "no London Parliament could have found the time or the knowledge for that transformation" of Ireland, and could pen verses of "Remorse for Intemperate Speech," he continued to delight in being intemperate. Just one year before he died he projected a periodical which he described to his friend Dorothy Wellesley as "an amusing thing to do—I shall curse my enemies" who will then "hit back and that will give me the joy of answering them." Only one number of *On the Boiler* appeared, posthumously. In it he adopted the role of the mad old ship's carpenter who delivered his harangues from a boiler on the Sligo quays. He attacked vulgarity wherever he saw it, or thought he saw it, and advocated a government by the elite. He went down fighting to the last, and that should win the respect of any Irishman.

Seldom has a nation found such an eloquent voice. He had dreamed of an ideal Ireland, and he had lived to see the birth of a new Ireland, different in many ways from that of his own proud imaginings. Yet, despite its shortcomings in comparison to a romantic isle of heroes, it was an Ireland of stirring memories. His last poems recapitulate the themes—his father at the Playboy debate, Maud Gonne with her statuesque carriage, the "gallant gentleman" Roger Casement, and Parnell, who had "loved a lass." Like those who died in 1916, Yeats lived so that Ireland's "heart mount up on high."

The gradual reconstruction of the country during the last thirty years has seemed an anticlimax to the dramatic events of earlier days. Independence has been won for the Southern counties, and the partition of the island is such an old and apparently unsolvable problem that it no longer arouses heat. There has been a steady improvement in the national economy, although emigration continues at the rate of about forty thousand persons a year. In the light of its bitter history, the most remarkable achievement has been the maintenance of religious toleration. But an Ireland without problems is almost inconceivable. Many have been the complaints about cultural insularity and sterility, and, on the other hand, about the loss of vitality in the native culture. For some time state censorship, and the even more insidious forms of suppression by parochial opinion, seemed to threaten Irish culture. In recent years, however, a more enlightened view has obtained, and works of unquestioned literary merit have been removed from the list of banned books. More debatable is the problem of the language. There is occasion for genuine concern at the death of Irish as a living language. The number of native speakers is declining at a rapid rate, and thirty-five years of official promotion have seemingly failed of their purpose, either because of the rapidity of the attempted shift from English to Irish or because of the effects of governmental pressure. To create a small Gaelic nation in the midst of an English-speaking world has seemed anachronistic and futile, although admirers of the poetry, eloquence, and wit of their linguistic inheritance cannot help but regret its loss. The generation of the patriot-idealists has all but disappeared, and once more Ireland faces the prospect of defining its place in the greatly changed mid-century world.

A remarkable feature of modern Irish history is the growing stature of Eamon de Valera during the 1930's and 1940's. Few national leaders have survived so much hatred and ridicule. His lean figure and unsmiling face made him a target for cartoonists. His policies have been met with derision. When he attacked the Treaty he was accused of word-splitting, and in the Civil War that followed he seemed guilty of fomenting anarchy. These were the wilderness years. Once hunted by the British, he was now pursued and imprisoned by the Irish of both North Ireland and the Free State. In fact he was a virtual outlaw, rejected by the I.R.A. and Sinn Fein alike. At this time, as Sean O'Faolain once observed, he, with his unkempt look, long overcoat, crushed felt hat, and worn brief case, might have been mistaken for any of the thousands of disheveled idealists and misfits who drifted throughout mid-European capitals. But his five and one-half years of political exile, fourteen months of them in prison, were finally ended. In August, 1927, he led his newly formed Fianna Fail party back into the Dail, at the cost of signing the hated oath of allegiance to the English crown. When he explained that he considered a compulsory oath not binding, he was mocked as an opportunist. On his assumption of leadership in 1932, many feared the possibility of a native fascism, and expected that he would retaliate upon his former enemies. His maintenance of neutrality during World War II, popular though it was in Ireland, was cynically attacked in England and America.

None of the labels has stuck, and few of the fears have materialized. With a dignity that confutes his mockers, de Valera has emerged as a Lincoln who survived the dramatic years of crisis and who has undertaken the drab duties of national recovery. As an obscure mathematics teacher he surprised everyone by becoming one of the most capable commanders in the 1916 Rising. The only leader to survive, he has remained in office ever since, with the exception of his abstention of 1922–27 and the two interludes of 1948–51 and 1954–57. But for millions the world over, de Valera, whether in or out of office, represents the Republic of Ireland.

A practical Quixote and a doctrinaire without vindictiveness, he has faced withering criticism without losing his equanimity. What confounds his opponents is the fact that he means what he says—although many complain that it is impossible to know just what he does say, his verbal ambiguities being notorious. To his scholastic mentality compromise is anathema, and he pursued his goal of a united, independent Ireland to the very brink of defeat before deflecting his course. His dogged persistence provided one of the rare instances of humor in his career. During the elections of 1923 he had been arrested at a meeting in the town of Ennis just as he was about to speak. One year later he was released, and returning to Ennis to speak, he opened with the casual phrase, "As I was saying to you when we were interrupted . . . ."

Utterly devoid of the romantic flamboyance that seems so characteristic of the Irish, his only shortcomings appear to be his virtues. He once admitted that his great strength was that he lacked the ability to say anything clever, "a fatal gift." This great abstainer does not smoke, does not drink, and does not engage in trivial talk. It has been said that he creates a drab image of peasant piety, but the image is also one of integrity and dedication. He has been accused of looking backward, of seeing in Ireland only a haven of provincial and unprogressive contentment. In any case, his values seem to be simple and refreshingly old-fashioned. He has been too honest to be diplomatic. When an applicant for a position on the *Irish Press* admitted to being unpolitically minded, the President of the Executive Council disarmingly replied, somewhat ruefully, "Neither am I." Yet the master politician Lloyd George said of de Valera's protest against the oath, "It is a clear demand from which Mr. de Valera has never swerved," adding, "He is that type; he will never change."

As head of the Council of the League of Nations in 1932, de Valera confounded experienced diplomats with his clear demands for disarmament. His opinion of Field Marshal Wilson's assassination in 1922 had been direct and honest: "I do not approve, but I must not pretend to misunderstand." It took courage, or obstinacy if you will, to maintain neutrality in World War II, for it meant closing Irish ports to Americans as well as to British. Yet when Winston Churchill, in his victory broadcast, indulged in self-congratulations on his "restraint and poise" in not forcing Ireland to concur, and referred to the shamefulness of Irish policy, de Valera made a dignified answer. Knowing, he said, the kind of reply that was expected, indeed the kind of reply that he himself might have made years before, "I shall strive not to be guilty of adding any fuel to the flames of hatred and passion, which, if continued to be fed, promise to burn up whatever is left by the war of decent human feelings in Europe." In the searing light of Churchill's rhetoric, these words seem colorless, but they are words of wisdom. Ireland's tempestuous struggles have ceased, and the dramatic gesture is no longer in fashion, but in the annals of history this clerical idealist will take his place beside his more vivid predecessors. Unlike them, he has not given his countrymen the customary memorable phrases and grand deeds. In fact it might be said that he has brought them little but that rarest of all features of Irish political life—success.

V - Humor

OF Dublin's many distinctions, possibly the most nearly unique is that of impromptu conversation, the most spontaneous and evanescent of the arts. Oscar Wilde comes to mind, although the brittle epigrams which have been preserved capture little of the fragile beauty and Mozartean grace which eager listeners found in his anecdotes. An elegant play of fancy is found in his comedies, where a rococo artificiality invests plot, character, and dialogue. A young drama critic, one George Bernard Shaw, hailed Wilde as the first true playwright, in that he plays with everything, actor and audience alike. In his extravaganzas Wilde evokes a sequence of shimmering illusions. Reality seems left far behind, until a sudden satiric stroke brings out the ironic relevance. His anecdotes must have been minor masterpieces. The cumulative effect of his wit can be tested in his comment on journalists. Condescendingly turning his definition into a rhetorical question, Wilde created a sentence masterful in its poise and perfect in rhythmic balance. Paradoxes are pointed by alliteration, and the final devastating thrust is the culmination of a long-delayed climax: "Who are these scribes who, passing with purposeless alacrity from the police news to the Parthenon, and from crime to criticism, sway with such serene incapacity the office which they so lately swept."

In warbling his native word-notes, Wilde never seemed to tire. He could turn a platitude inside out, and reveal a brilliant truth. His insouciance was at hand when a blackmailer demanded ten pounds for an incriminating letter. "Ten pounds!" Wilde exclaimed. "You have no appreciation of literature. If you had asked me for fifty pounds I might have given it." After being tried and convicted on a charge of sodomy in 1895, as he was being transferred to prison, he once had to stand on a train platform, handcuffed, amid a jeering crowd. The experience was so humiliating that every afternoon thereafter he wept in his cell at this time. Yet even as he stood there, he had been able to remark to his warden, "If this is the way Queen Victoria treats her convicts, she doesn't deserve to have any." In Reading Jail he made friends and entertained people, whether prisoners or officials. When he was asked whether Marie Corelli was a great writer, the reply was, "Now don't think I've anything against her *moral* character, but from the way she writes *she ought to be here.*"

Hesketh Pearson has complained that Wilde repeated many epigrams, but one at least gained by repetition, each variation revealing another delightful facet:

There are two ways of disliking poetry; one way is to dislike it, and the other is to like it rationally.

There are two ways of disliking poetry; one way is to dislike it, the other is to read Pope.

Humor

There are two ways of disliking my plays; one way is to dislike them, the other is to prefer *Earnest*.

Although the analyst of humor risks the absurdity of trying to account for the unaccountable, one may note that for centuries the Irish have delighted in the sheer play of the imagination. Wandering poets, if not hospitably treated on their travels, retaliated with satiric doggerel that echoed through the countryside—a sort of poetic blackmail. Several ninth-century Gaelic cats illustrate the antiquity of Irish whimsy. In the highly ornamented gospel manuscript, the *Book of Kells*, two white tabbies pose complacently in the margin of one page oblivious to the mouse on each other's back, so fascinated are they at two other mice tugging at a Communion wafer. Most famous of all cats is Pangur Ban, associate of the monk who, far from home, kept his commonplace book at the Abbey of St. Gall in Switzerland. His charming verse notes the resemblances between human and feline research:

> *I and Pangur Ban my cat,*
> *'Tis a like task we are at:*
> *Hunting mice is his delight,*
> *Hunting words I sit all night.*

For the other stanzas the reader is referred to *The Irish Tradition* (1947), a tour de force of imaginative historical reconstruction by Robin Flower. Not only cats, but hermits, bards, and missionaries are seen in their habits as they lived.

Every commentator, native or foreign, friendly or unfriendly, notes the Irishman's readiness of phrase and his use of metaphor in ordinary conversation, a quality of style exploited in the plays of Synge and O'Casey. "Lynn Doyle," in his fine study of *The Spirit of Ireland* (1935), argued that the Irish are not untruthful or insincere but must be regarded as artists who "do not relate life, they recreate it for our benefit." Even Tom Penhaligon, in his diatribe on *The Impossible Irish* (1935), grudgingly admits that "the Irish are always at their best when they have an audience," and that their imagination is such that "the world that means most to them is the world of make-believe." So too, did Stephen MacKenna, despite his sorrow at the moral collapse of his country in the "troubles," exclaim in a letter of Christmas Eve, 1923, that, whatever can be said against the Irish, "by heavens we're eloquent: the beautiful words are a joy, and what is more remarkable still is the sense of conversation . . . an exquisite art, practised with love and fury, and warmly appreciated," which one finds in people of all ages. In England, on the other hand, during seven months he had heard "never a fresh phrase, never a newly coined combination of pleasant sound such as I hear all day around me in my own Dundrum."

Ireland's trilingual tradition of Gaelic, English, and Latin, together with the academic and scholastic mentality developed in parochial education, leads to poems and puns in several languages, the macaronic mode of the Middle Ages. These forms of humor are still popular in Ireland on the music-hall level and, in a more recondite style, in the sonorous mysteries of Joyce's giant enigma *Finnegans Wake*. English transliterations of Gaelic place-names offer a constant temptation to the linguistic humorist; there are "Bally" (town), "Boy" (yellow), "Cool" (corner), "Glas" (green), "Kill" (church), or "Knock" (hill), to select a few.

The joke "I've been to Kilmany and I'm going to Kilmore" is at least two hundred years old.

An important factor in Irish humor is its value as an escape from otherwise intolerable situations. The "gallows humor" of Ireland appears in such popular ballads as "The Night before Larry Was Stretched," depicting a farewell card game and drinking party given for a condemned man on the night before his hanging. The imperturbable Larry pays no attention to repentance; and as for hanging, he indulges in an Irish bull—of all methods of dying there's "the devil a betther a-livin'!" Equally popular is the macabre description of the return of a mutilated war veteran, "Johnny, I Hardly Knew Ye," verses which stimulated the impulse toward parody of at least two distinguished Dubliners, the Trinity don Robert Yelverton Tyrrell and Oliver St. John Gogarty.

The revolt of the intellectual who, like Stephen Dedalus in *A Portrait of the Artist*, will not serve that which he cannot believe has its verbal expression in epigram and paradox. Christianity itself is based on paradox, or rather on a series of paradoxical reversals of worldly values, as Hugh Kenner has demonstrated in his study of G. K. Chesterton. Mysteries of the spirit are not capable of rational resolution; if they can be destroyed by logic, they can be demonstrated by life.

In the *Spectator* essays, Joseph Addison, in so many ways Victorian a century before Victoria, labored to establish polite taste in contemporary fashion. During one week in early May, 1711, his essays were devoted to false wit in its various forms of figured verse (recently revived by Dylan Thomas), anagrams, acrostics, doggerel, and puns. One is happy to report that he had the greatest difficulty in exorcising the pun, for he had to admit that "The Seeds of Punning are in the Minds of all Men, and tho' they may be subdued by Reason, Reflection, and good Sense, they will be very apt to shoot up in the greatest Genius." Addison's authority has been influential, but fortunately not definitive. Puns may be defended on the same basis as cakes and ale, that is, for sheer delight, but if a more serious defense be sought, it may be found implicit in James Joyce's reply to a query whether his puns weren't trivial: "Some of them are trivial and some are quadrivial." The reference to the scholastic curriculum suggests the relationships between departmentalized forms of knowledge, and the role of language as a somewhat adequate but often faulty mode of communication. A Jesuit scholar who has made an authoritative study of *Joyce and Aquinas* (1957), Rev. William T. Noon, points out that the pun is a metaphor which "the phonetic or orthographic accident fortuitously, as it were, highlights or 'sparks' with energy."

In answer to Addison one could point out that man confronts the inconsecutiveness of life, its existential absurdity, with humor and irony. That English master of irony, Thomas Hardy, defined it in the title to a group of poems, "Satires of Circumstance." In the irony of fate it is as though fate gives the mocking lie to human plans and human dreams. But man in turn is able to mock the mocker; he can laugh at the disorder of existence, and he can laugh at the inadequacy of human forms of order. One of the vehicles of order is language. The epigram, the paradox, and the Irish bull might be called ordered forms of disorder, filled with false clues of statement and of sound. Just as Hamlet is both distracted and protected by wild and whirling words, so the Irish may have compensated for their historical disasters by their eminence in verbal warfare. Thus in his reminiscences Oliver St. John Gogarty delights in the triumph of his own imagination: "How magnificently I was turning the tables on reality by making it wax and wane to suit my ebb and flow of consciousness."

The Irish bull, a logical statement of an absurdity, illustrates the inextricable confusion of order and disorder. The witty classicist Mahaffy defined the Irish bull as the only bull that is pregnant, and Lynn Doyle's definition, like Mahaffy's, is itself a bull: "The saying of a thing in an obscure way to make your meaning clearer than if you had put it in plain language." To illustrate, one may quote the politician who asserted that "half the lies the Nationalists tell the people are not true."

As a master of satiric invective, Jonathan Swift exploited every shade of tonal modulation, ranging from pretended indifference to the utmost vituperation. Gulliver's experiences provide a compendium of rhetorical devices, which analytical critics and readers alike never cease to enjoy. To mention only a few in passing, there is the fiction of the innocent observer who merely reports what he sees, and, in the first two books of the *Travels*, the toying with perspective through which human affairs are seen in Lilliputian triviality and then projected in their gigantic enormity. The manipulation of understatement and overstatement, the flights into the absurd, and the descents into the scatological may also be mentioned.

Analysis of the clever involutions of Swift's satiric genius can be more readily encompassed by outlining the main turns of thought in his defense of Christianity. The elaborate title is permeated with innuendo: "An Argument to prove that the Abolishing of Christianity in England may, as things now stand, be attended with some inconveniences, and perhaps not produce those many good effects proposed thereby." Note the cautious and revealing modification, "as things now stand," the understatement, "some inconveniences," and the hypothetical proposal which is to be refuted. The primary supposition that men wish to abolish Christianity is based on the way they act. Thus it may seem paradoxical, even in this paradoxical age, to try to defend something so outmoded. Yet, imprudent as that be, Swift hastens to reassure us that he is not so foolish as to attempt to defend real Christianity. Any such effort "would indeed be a wild project," which, if successful, would have utterly devastating effects upon "the entire frame and constitution of things," such as trade, learning, courts, exchanges, and shops. The arguments for abolishing nominal Christianity may seem unanswerable: its impossible demands on faith, and even more impossible demands on conduct, would lead one to believe that there would be less faction and more comfort without the church. No one, however, is really inconvenienced by these demands nowadays, and there is "one darling inclination of mankind" which can be counted on to keep faction alive, namely, the spirit of opposition. If the wits were not able to attack the church, things might get out of hand indeed, what with the disturbance of the peace and the breaking of laws. Then too, religion has some value to the common people, "as furnishing excellent material to keep children quiet when they grow peevish, and providing topics of amusement in a tedious winter-night." Practical objections to the cost and time spent on religion can be similarly answered. Few people are really bothered. The crowning inconveniences of abolishing Christianity remain to be mentioned. It "may perhaps bring the Church into danger, or at least put the senate to the trouble of another securing vote." It could affect our alliances; and, worst of all, "I do very much apprehend, that in six months time after the act is passed . . . the Bank, and East-India Stock, may fall at least one *per cent*." Since this is fifty times more than we spend to preserve the church, it would be folly to incur "so great a loss, merely for the sake of destroying it."

If the prose displays the grand effects of irony, Swift's poetry shows the lighter side of his verbal agility. In his "Serious Poem" ridiculing William Wood, the promoter of the hated coinage of 1724, Swift romps through dozens of puns on the name. He proclaims that "we all should Rejoyce to be *Hewers* of WOOD," toys with the idea of using faggots to burn "an old Fryer," speculates on what species the coiner might be—"*Son of a BEECH*," thorn, crab, or poison yew—and raises the embarrassing question:

> *How came it to pass*
> *WOOD got so much Copper? He got it by BRASS* . . . .

With his cronies Delany and Sheridan, Swift exchanged riddles and epigrams, occasional verse, even a parody cantata. He used triple rhyme in an invitation to Sheridan:

> *Dear Tom, this verse, which however the beginning may*
> *   appear, yet in the* end's good metre,
> *Is sent to desire that, when your August vacation comes,*
> *   your* friend's you'd meet here . . . .

He can repeat identical double rhymes ad infinitum:

I pitied my Cat, whom I knew by her Mew sick;
She mended at first, but now she's anew sick.
Captain Butler made some in the Church black and blue
*   sick*
Dean Cross, had he preach'd, would have made us all
*   Pew-sick . . . .*

His mock Latin is most amusing, especially in the charming verses to Molly:

> *Mollis abuti,*
> *Has an acuti*
> *No lasso finis;*
> *Molli dii vinis . . . .*

Although Queen Victoria's best-known words were "We
are not amused," her long reign saw the heyday of verbal
humor. Comic magazines and light opera helped relieve
the monotony of respectability. England produced Gilbert and Sullivan and Lewis Carroll, and the Irish joined
in the fun. A strange sequence of parody upon parody has
been recounted by Mr. Vivien Mercier in one of his essays
on Irish humor. The doggerel of "Castlehyde" makes it a
worthy candidate for the title of one of the worst poems in
English. Its jingling rhythms have been attributed to an
Irish poet's imperfect knowledge of English poetic idiom:

The richest groves throughout this nation and fine plan-
*   tations you will see there;*
The rose, the tulip, and sweet carnation, all vying with
*   the lily fair.*

Richard Milliken once won a bet that he could write
something equally absurd. The result was "The Groves of

Blarney." The game was on, and the unconventional priest and wit of *Fraser's Magazine*, Father Mahony, added stanzas, as well as inventing a Greek "original" and Italian, French, and Latin versions! This master mixer of languages and predecessor of James Joyce, through his creation "Father Prout," carried on a literary feud with the popular Irish versifier Tom Moore. His essay on "The Rogueries of Tom Moore" accused the poet of plagiarism through the dubious expedient of praising his translations from French, Latin, and Greek "sources," all of them of course created by Mahony himself. After all, he said, translation "is the next best thing to having a genius of one's own." But when the translations are praised as almost equal to the presumed originals, we are in the looking-glass world of Sterne or Joyce!

Father Mahony had the unusual distinction of having been discharged from his position at the school later attended by Joyce, Clongowes Wood College. It seems that on an outing he and his charges imbibed so freely that they returned strapped to loads of turf in carts! He once characterized himself as "an Irish potato seasoned with Attic salt," and said of Father Prout what he might just as well have said of himself that "his brain was a storehouse of inexhaustible knowledge, and his memory a bazaar."

His equal as a linguist and wit was his colleague William Maginn, the editor of *Fraser's Magazine*. Maginn once supplied elegiac verses for Sir Daniel Donnelly in Greek, Latin, and Hebrew, and fabricated others by "Byron" and "Wordsworth." A contemporary London editor, William Jerden of the *Literary Gazette*, admitted the impossibility of conveying the temperament of Maginn, "the precocious, the prolific, the humorous, the eccentric, the erratic, the versatile, the learned, the wonderfully endowed, the Irish."

The remarks of the genial classicist Tyrrell are still remembered. He once drily observed that there was no such thing as a large whisky, and claimed that a temperance hotel was a contradiction in terms. When his colleague Mahaffy stopping preaching at Trinity, Tyrrell claimed that he began to be afflicted with insomnia at morning chapel.

Trinity College, Dublin, has seen strange sights. It has seen Mahaffy preach and the entertainer Percy French study engineering, and finally graduate, so he said, because the authorities were afraid that he might become eligible for a pension. As for Mahaffy, Gogarty, who has described him so often and so well, called him "the Most Magnificent of Snobs." When this thoroughgoing rationalist was approached by an eager evangelical enthusiast with the usual question, "Are you saved?" his answer was one to turn away enthusiasm: "To tell you the truth, my dear fellow, I am, but it was by such a narrow squeak that it won't bear discussing."

Percy French staged the Irishman in song and skit, and made himself beloved at the same time. He once explained his secret by saying that he was "born a boy and . . . remained one ever since." One of his most popular comic recitations, "The Four Farrellys," mimics the accent and characteristics of typical Ulster, Munster, Leinster, and Connacht men. The song-and-dance routine of "Phil the Fluter's Ball" describes the expedient through which this vagrant gained a living by passing a hat to the accompaniment of jig and flute. Its imitative patter made it memorable, and title and text find their way into Joyce's extravaganza *Finnegans Wake,* which, incidentally, derives from another music-hall song. The "Four-an'-twinty fightin' min" of "Shlathery's Mounted Fut" are every bit as memorable.

Among the classics of modern Irish humor a place must be found for Lennox Robinson's delightful comedy of maternal love and indulgence, *The Whiteheaded Boy* (1916). The family circle, indeed a great part of the community, finds itself inextricably involved in the destinies of the playboy who is unable to pass his medical examinations at Trinity. The play is as universally loved as its principal character, and as well adapted to the stage as its famed predecessors in the comedy of manners, the popular favorites of Goldsmith and Sheridan, who, incidentally, were Irish too.

There is the strangely macabre humor of Seumas O'Kelly's long story *The Weaver's Grave* (1919), a minor masterpiece of mingled pathos and comedy in which two aged men stumble through an ill-kept graveyard in search of a burial place. As they mumble to themselves and argue with each other, the grotesquerie of the human condition is made apparent—and also, in an odd way, something of its grandeur. Here peasant humor is deepened into a realization of the state in which all, rich and poor, educated or rustic, meet at last on the same level. What might have been a sentimental episode becomes, in O'Kelly's skillful telling, a tragically moving tale. One is reminded of the humanity displayed in many of the pictures of common life by Jack Butler Yeats. In both painter and storyteller, humor and humanity meet to form a poignant expression of mood, and it was natural that Yeats was chosen to illustrate an edition of O'Kelly's story, just as he had earlier illustrated Synge's sketches of *The Aran Islands*.

By his witty speeches in the English Parliament, Tim Healy overcame much of the unpopularity that stemmed from his earlier defection from Parnell. Diarmuid Russell reprints two of his classic utterances in *The Portable Irish Reader* (1946). At the time when the Boer War was becoming almost as unpopular in England as it had been in Ireland, Healy charged that "You want to syndicate Christianity, and take the Twelve Apostles into your limited liability company." Laudable as it may be to have other nations contemplate your virtues, a privilege already enjoyed by the Irish, the English should realize that the Dutch in South Africa are not so near, and that "misunderstandings may crop up." Unlike the Irish, the South Africans do not have the advantages "of seeing the British constantly, of reading your newspapers, and chanting Rudyard Kipling"—an author, by the way, "whom it is extremely difficult to translate into Dutch."

The Irish have found Kipling an ideal target. A people with a long religious tradition, they can easily unmask the penny's worth of gospel in these jungle tunes. The pompous platitudes will not escape a nation long misruled by the English. It is not hard to strip the robes of piety from this sanctimonious imperialist. And to compound the aggravation, Kipling was himself of Ulster stock and had written a blatant warning against the fury of Irish Catholics, "the hells declared/ For such as serve not Rome." Of those who have taken Kipling's measure, none were more successful than Susan Mitchell, who adapted the banalities of "Recessional" to the pleading of an Ulster Protestant having "a few plain words" with the Deity. The well-known refrain is modified into a gibe at the bourgeois traits for which Northern Ireland has long been ridiculed, the Deity being appraised of the fact that "our hearts are set/ On what we get, on what we get." Then, most recently, there is the free adaptation of Kipling in Brendan Behan's sarcastic song extolling English virtues, with its inane refrain, "The captains and the kings." This jingle pops into Behan's theatrical extravaganza *The Hostage* (1958) with the same unpredictability as do most of the characters.

Susan Mitchell's delicious mockery is contained in the little volume *Aids to the Immortality of Certain Persons in Ireland, Charitably Administered* (1908). The author provides her own review of the book, so that no reviewer may "wriggle in" between poet and "victim." The verses are topical, centering around George Moore's antics, the rising force of Sinn Fein, the controversies over the Municipal Art Gallery, and the riots at the performance of Synge's *The Playboy of the Western World*. A ballad which brings in many Dublin characters is that of John Shawe-Taylor and Hugh Lane, concerning the presumedly forged early Corot in Lane's collection:

> *Æ was there with his long hair,*
> *And Orpen, R.H.A.*
> *Sir Thomas Drew was in a stew,*
> *And looked the other way . . . .*

Others were present:

> *And John B. Yeats stood near the gates,*
> *With mischief in his gaze,*
> *While W. B., the poet, he*
> *Pondered a telling phrase;*

You'll find it in the Freeman
After a day or so . . . .

Misunderstood as a libel on Ireland, Synge's contro-versial *The Playboy of the Western World* is itself a gem of humorous insights. The central situation, that of the admiration bestowed by country girls on a supposed mur-derer, is a poetic fantasy on the imagination and its de-sire for romantic escape—Irish perhaps, but universal as well. The gentle humor of the characterization is equaled by the poetry of the dialogue. An invalid himself, Synge extolled life, and the love of life shines brightly through this masterpiece.

It is easy to see that the audience, blinded by political and moral sentimentality, could rise in righteous indigna-tion against the play. On the first night, when the hero made his vividly metaphorical expression of preference for Pegeen, hisses and catcalls broke out and not another word could be heard. "It's Pegeen I'm seeking only," Christy exclaimed, "an what'd I care if you brought me a drift of chosen females, standing in their shifts itself, may-be, from this place to the eastern world." Victoria had been dead only six years, and to Victorian sensibilities these words might arouse response in other places as well as in Ireland. As the week went on, audiences were increasingly unruly. Tempers were not cooled by the appearance, on the second night, of the hated Metropolitan Police, nor by a tactless remark made by Yeats regarding the "com-monplace and ignorant people" who controlled patriotic clubs and societies. Nevertheless, the play ran for one week, and a public debate was staged on the freedom of the theatre. With his usual flair for the dramatic, Yeats an-

nounced himself: "The author of 'Cathleen ni Houlihan'
appeals to you," thus mentioning the major patriotic success of the theatre.

Yet even this row stirred the health-giving winds of
mockery. *The Abbey Row, NOT Edited by W. B. Yeats,*
a parody of the theater journal *The Arrow,* is still delightful to read. On the cover, the Abbey emblem of Cuchulain
and his wolfhound is replaced by a caricature of Mrs.
Grundy holding in tow a dog with the face of Synge. The
narrative is illustrated by cartoons and interrupted by
verse parodies, concluding with a ballad that sums up
the affair:

> *A dramatist once wrote a play*
>   *About an Irish peasant,*
> *We heard some of the audience say*
>   *"The motive is not pleasant."*
> *Our own opinion, we admit,*
>   *Is rather—well—uncertain,*
> *Because we couldn't hear one bit*
>   *From rise to fall of curtain . . . .*

Among other amusing tidbits, the word in Synge's play
which inflamed the audience was memorialized by Susan
Mitchell:

> *Oh, no, we never mention it, its name is never heard—*
> *New Ireland sets its face against the once familiar word.*
> *They take me to the Gaelic League where men wear*
>   *kilts, and yet*
> *The simple word of childhood's days I'm bidden to*
>   *forget!*

And, in the concluding stanza:

Then by those early memories, hearken to one who prays
The right to mention once again the word of other days,
Without Police Protection once more her voice to lift—
The right to tell (even to herself) that still she wears—
  a shift!

In *The Crock of Gold* (1912) the iridescent imagination of James Stephens plays upon talkative and silent philosophers, old women with stones in their boots, and children whose eyes are being awakened to the beauty of existence. This fantasy is deservedly one of the most popular of Irish books. As a poet, Stephens is equally original. Fairies and satyrs and stamping centaurs, soaring birds and the apple at the very end of the bough make his verses little philosophic fables of the love of life. There is technical virtuosity too, as in "Arpeggio," a sequence of dancing lines only one or two syllables long, or in the thirteen-line apostrophe—without a verb—of "The Main Deep":

> *. . . long-rolling*
> *Steady-pouring*
> *Deep trenched . . . .*

Of Stephens, Æ might well have said what he wrote in tribute to Gogarty, that his poetry, "the opposite of my own," conveys "some gay and gallant life which was not in my own birthright." More strident than Stephens, Gogarty treats classic myth with coy innuendo, picturing Helen of Troy first putting up her hair, the young Leda shyly bathing, and the Girton Girls of Sappho's isle. Gogarty's epigrams, limericks, and audacious verse had long been known in Dublin. One of George Moore's regrets at leaving Ireland in 1911 was separation from his youngest friend, described in *Vale* as "the arch mocker, the author of all the jokes that enable us to live in Dublin," the surgeon with "a smile in his eyes and always a witticism on his lips, overflowing with quotation."

Gogarty published little under his own name until after his dramatic escape from kidnapers during the period of terrorism in the Civil War. Taken as a hostage—he was a senator at the time—he jumped into the Liffey and swam to safety. His thank-offering of swans to the river gave another anecdote to Dublin and a title to his first volume of verse, *An Offering of Swans* (1924). Yeats, his fellow senator, wrote a gracious introduction, remarking the transformation of a wit into a poet.

Gogarty's wit is apparent in the anonymous collection of humorous verse, *Secret Springs of Dublin Song* (1918). Here are the usual parodies—the ballad of "Johnny, I Hardly Knew Ye" as it might have been written by Swinburne or Milton, and the Latin version of "Little Jack Horner." Here also is an unusual invocation to spring, the tempting streetwalker who:

> *. . . comes tripping down the street,*
> *And not a Bobbie on his beat*
> *Can hold her up, or stop the Spring*
> *From shamelessly soliciting—*
> *Even the Vigilance Committee*
> *Can't keep the Spring from Dublin City.*

And it must surely be Gogarty who in "The Isles of Greece" extols a hearty sailor who doesn't give a damn for those renowned lands. His directness, the poet notes, "is vitalising/ After years of Arnoldising." In toasting him who "thus lay bare of myths/ Ionian thalattaliths," the anonymous writer seems to call up the spirit of James Joyce, who was to do that very thing in *Ulysses*.

Joyce's humor ranges from subtle irony to boisterous horseplay. The verbal mockery in *Ulysses* and *Finnegans Wake* seems inexhaustible in its Rabelaisian gusto. Nothing is spared—not even the reader. Joyce is magpie and mockingbird. No style and no subject is immune to his parody. This Irishman is too Irish for the Irish, and he does not hesitate to foul his own nest.

The irony that pervades the *Dubliners* stories is more conventional. A terror-stricken child, escaping from his father's brutality, promises to say a "Hail, Mary" for his undeserving parent; a man who has brought on the suicide of an unhappy woman congratulates himself on his own virtue; a priest, addressing a businessmen's group, suggests that his audience settle their spiritual accounts.

Yet this man loved Ireland, and his view of the human race is far from nihilistic. In *Ulysses*, Molly Bloom is notorious for unabashed sexuality, yet she has, beneath her vulgarity, a longing for beauty and love. The triumph of Joyce's art is the creation of the pathetic and ridiculous sidewalk Quixote, the middle-aged Leopold Bloom. His mind is a lumber room of misinformation, romantic longing, and Walter Mitty dreams of success. Although we are amused and insulted by this travesty of humanity, a sober second thought brings us to an awareness of our own blood-brotherhood. And in the end the portrait is not quite so unflattering, for Bloom has a deeper humanity than we had realized. This Chaplin-like quality was conveyed with astonishing success by the actor Zero Mostel in the dramatization of *Ulysses in Nighttown* which proved to be unexpectedly popular off Broadway in 1958 and later played in London, Paris, and The Hague. His moon-faced, featureless, and paunchy Bloom will not be forgotten soon.

For seventeen years James Joyce devoted his linguistic facility and his extraordinary powers of association to the writing of *Finnegans Wake* (1939). It is an epic based on a music-hall tune, a polyglot parody of history, a tender evocation of the cycle of life. It is also a work which few can read and fewer understand. Considered a hoax by the unsympathetic, a monstrous failure by the frustrated, and a masterpiece by the elite, *Finnegans Wake* is the most elaborately contrived work in modern literature. Two things are clear. Primarily, it is funny; the text is a tissue of mocking echoes. Thousands of familiar phrases are chopped up into strange shapes in this Irish stew. Secondly, as the recent dramatization of selected episodes has made clear, it is scored for voices—and Irish voices at that. Staged as *The Voice of Shem,* the adaptation was the outstanding hit of the 1961 Theatre Festival in Dublin. The warring sons, Shem and Shaun, make a perfect music-hall team. Shem, the slight tenor, modeled on Joyce himself, is the victim of the insults hurled by the dark, round-faced Dublin gallant, a type that has delighted audiences for generations with casual impertinences and good-humored disrespect.

There are solos, such as the self-justification of the tavern-keeper Everybody, as he faces or imagines he faces nameless and countless accusers. There is the touching farewell of the mother-figure Anna Livia, as she turns at last to extinction in the sea and rebirth in the cloud—for this eternal feminine is the water of life and also the River Liffey as it flows past Adam's and Eve's Church to the Irish Sea. The associations with Eden, Dublin, woman, and life are typically Joycean.

VI - The Achievement

IN December, 1921—the time of the Anglo-Irish Treaty
—Valéry Larbaud gave a prepublication lecture on James
Joyce's forthcoming novel *Ulysses*. He correctly predicted
that with it Ireland was about to make a sensational re-
entry into the main stream of European literature. The
French critic could have added the example of Yeats,
whose poems of this period the world will not soon forget.
If by some mischance the Irish literary revival had ended
in 1914, it would now be regarded as a pleasant but not too
important byway in literary history, somewhat like the
Pre-Raphaelite movement, which also had stimulated the
sister arts of painting and poetry. With the sole exception
of Synge's plays, none of the Irish masterpieces had appeared. Thus far Joyce had been represented only by the
delicate poems of *Chamber Music* (1907) and the stories
of *Dubliners* (1914). Reviews of *Dubliners* were dwarfed
by headlines about Sarajevo; the year 1914, the end of a
chapter in European history, was not without political

172

and cultural significance in Ireland. It is with a strangely accidental appositeness that the four principal accounts of the early Irish revival came out at this time—George Moore's *Hail and Farewell* (1911–14), Lady Gregory's *Our Irish Theatre* (1913), Cornelius Weygandt's *Irish Plays and Playwrights* (1913), and Ernest Boyd's *Irish Literary Renaissance* (1916).

On hearing of such feats of improvisation as Æ's extraordinary ability to dash off a poem or a picture in a matter of moments, or Stephen MacKenna's impromptu conversational powers, one may recall Wilde's remark about his countrymen being "too poetical to be poets," and conclude that fluency is the Irishman's fatal gift. Many have been, like George Bernard Shaw, fellows of infinite jest, but, alas, where are now their quillets and quiddities? Irish literature has displayed in abundance the conversational values of spontaneity and originality, less often the classic disciplines of incisiveness and finality. Shaw's Puritan severity extended to wine, women, and song, but never to words or ideas. Insights tumble one after another, flashes of wit blaze and coruscate. Plot is long since forgotten, and soon character, episode, and even audience are overlooked in the excitement of the chase. The play at last concluded, the prefaces begin, and after the prefaces the notes, the postscripts, and the retrospective essays.

In the midst of his diverse activities Yeats always held before himself the ideal: "Hammer your thoughts into unity." For European culture he had the same goal, hoping that Ireland might show the way by turning from the "bragging rhetoric and gregarious humour" of earlier days to the ideal represented by Parnell, "solitary and proud." Certainly Yeats's own career gained strength through its unified development, in which speeches and essays document plays and poems, and youthful concerns mature and burgeon, rising from the personal domain to the national, and finally to the universal plane. One of his favorite images of organic growth was the tree. In accounting for the literary failure of his father's friend John Todhunter, Yeats detected a lack of passion and the absence of harmonious growth: "If he had liked anything strongly he might have been a famous man, for a few years later he was to write, under some casual patriotic impulse, certain excellent verses now in all Irish anthologies; but with him every book was a new planting, and not a new bud on an old bough."

In a poetic career, it is almost impossible to overcome the handicap of early success. Anthologies, from *Tottel's Miscellany* of 1557, have been memorials to minor talents. Yeats, happily, was one of the few exceptions, a man who triumphed over success. He started as a minor poet not unlike Todhunter. "The Lake Isle of Innisfree," those lines that he might willingly have let die, so weary he was of being tied to them, could well be described as "certain excellent verses now in all Irish anthologies." But from this slender stalk, what a deeply rooted and fully laden tree!

At the peak of his success as a "Celtic" poet, Yeats realized the necessity of giving up the facile lyricism he had perfected. He wrote a letter of apology to Æ in 1904, excusing some tactless comments he had made on the poems in the latter's *New Songs*. If he had been less than fair, he candidly admitted, it was because he saw in them "an exaggeration of sentiment and sentimental beauty which I have come to think unmanly," and which he had been striving to overcome in his own work. His postscript concludes with the triumphant assertion, "Let us have no emotions, however abstract, in which there is not an athletic joy."

Style was one means of escaping facility. Yeats noted that the work of Douglas Hyde suffered because he never realized the necessity of writing English like a learned language. Synge's famous preface to his own *The Playboy of the Western World* urged that "in a good play every speech should be as fully flavored as nut or apple." In Trieste, Joyce was at the same time recasting the manuscript of *Stephen Hero* to transform it from an episodic autobiography to the classically unified novel, *A Portrait of the Artist as a Young Man.* Yeats was often attacked for his revisions. In the 1908 collected edition of his works he answered his critics in an epigram. Its concluding line, "It is myself that I remake," sums up his self-conscious artistry.

In the library scene of Joyce's *Ulysses*, Stephen Dedalus discusses the art of Shakespeare and the mysteries of artistic creation. At one point he pontificates, "The man of genius makes no mistakes," for "his errors are volitional and are the portals of discovery." In his urgency to test anew each of his intuitions, Yeats gave the impression of having rejected positions which were only temporarily abandoned. Throughout his career he retained an almost unprecedented creative vitality. At intervals of a decade or so he displayed a phoenixlike power of imaginative renewal. Many times he revised and tightened his earlier work in preparation for another rebirth. Noting this phenomenon, he wrote to Mrs. Shakespear in February, 1934: "It is curious how one's life falls into definite sections. In

1897 a new scene was set, new actors appeared." The theatrical metaphors were appropriate, for Yeats was constantly aware of the division of his own personal drama into unified acts. This awareness accounts not only for the painstaking unity of each volume of poems but for the retention of publication dates in the collected work.

Thus nothing is lost in the Yeats canon. The frequently observed shifts of emphasis resemble the emergence and subsidence of a floating object. The passionate dances of the sages in the poem "Byzantium," a vision of the sixty-five-year-old poet, are prefigured in a ritual described thirty-five years before. In the esoteric tale of "Rosa Alchemica" initiates, robed in scarlet, trace in a mystic dance the pattern of the mosaic rose on the ceiling of their shrine. A companion story with cabalistic implications, "The Tables of the Law," contains a discussion of Byzantine motifs "that suggest an imagination absorbed in the contemplation of Eternity." The recluse and hermetic student Owen Aherne discusses the prophetic book by Joachim of Flora which predicts an era in which children of the Holy Spirit will create "that supreme art which is to win us from life and gather us into eternity." This is the theme, and these are the very words of the magnificent poem "Sailing to Byzantium."

Few sought so strenuously to plan their careers. With sensibility exercised by meditation, and mind stored with poetic tradition, Yeats centered his writing on basic themes, returning to them again and again with increasing power. With equal care he planned each volume as an artistic unit, arranging poems so as to link them by theme, mood, or image.

The Achievement

Ancient symbolism gave strength to Yeats's poetry. At once clear and evocative, heron or winding stair or golden bird need no scholarly gloss for the imaginative reader. If mankind did not "remember or half remember impossible things," he once said, "what Aran fisher-girl would sing?" In his meditations on the *Anima Mundi* (1917), or memory of humanity, Yeats rooted poetic and religious symbols in the beliefs and hopes of mankind. The concept of the racial unconscious postulated by Carl Jung finds little corroboration from anthropologists; tradition may result from environment rather than from inherited traits; nonetheless, the imaginations of men have turned in varied places and times to such natural symbols as mountain and sea, horse and bird, wind and cloud, to reflect their emotions. Yeats found that symbols enabled him to escape isolation "amid the obscure impressions of the senses." The amazing fact is that even his occult poetry is sharply etched. The authority is felt even though the meaning may not be entirely clear.

The rose and the tower are good examples of Yeats's poetic practice. Both emblems are traditional, having literary as well as historic associations—the rose with beauty, purity, and spirituality; the tower, as Yeats said, with "mysterious wisdom won by toil," as well as with nobility, ancient Ireland, and the poet's own fortified house in County Galway. Yeats used these and other equally public symbols as motifs in many poems. The rose provided a title for an early collection, *The Secret Rose* (1897), a book whose occult character is suggested by the elaborate gold design on the cover. An intricate tree of life, growing from a skeleton, branches into cabalistic roses. It blossoms into the faces of a man and a woman who kiss and clasp hands above a central cross. The designs of later volumes were less complex but designed with equal care.

A major portal of discovery was that of the fine arts. All readers can recall the procession of Magi, knights, dragons, dolphins, as well as numerous references to mosaic, portrait, altarpiece, and landscape. Yeats himself gave up painting after two years of training, but he never ceased to furnish his imagination with visual motifs, many of them discovered by Professor T. W. Henn and described in *The Lonely Tower* (1950). Two of his father's subjects, hunchback and laughing beggar, provided vehicles for poetry and prophecy. Like the fools in Shakespeare's plays, these vagrants, granted immunity from criticism, voice an irresponsible defiance that Yeats was hesitant to utter in his own person. In his interpretation of human destiny, *A Vision,* (1926), hunchback, saint, and fool again appear. They represent the three final phases of the twenty-eight character types described. Yeats's late, earthy ballads may derive their coarse and sardonic energy from the vigorous woodcuts and paintings of his brother Jack, which portray the activities of tinkers and carnival roustabouts.

The classic masterpieces of European art were intimately known by Yeats. He utilized such episodes as Leda and the Swan or Oedipus and the Sphinx, the Annuciation or the Adoration of the Magi. In his theory of history he found ancient sculpture and Byzantine mosaics evidence of waxing and waning subjectively. At one time he projected a lecture tour for which he prepared a file of slides including designs by William Blake, Samuel Palmer, and Edward Calvert.

The artists Edmund Dulac and T. Sturge Moore were

congenial co-workers. Dulac created costumes and masks for the private performance of Yeats's *At the Hawk's Well* in London (1916). For *A Vision*, Dulac designed a wood-cut representing the great wheel of the moon's phases, and one of a prancing unicorn, as well as a portrait of the ficti-tious medieval scholar Giraldus. Moore was a closer friend. Not only an artist, he was a poet who anticipated two Yeats poems, with a translation in 1893 of Ronsard's "When You Are Old" and two treatments of the Leda story in 1914, "To Leda" and "The Home of Helen." His woodcuts of candle, eagle, and unicorn descending from the stars were often used in the volumes published by the Yeats sisters at the Cuala Press. In his correspondence with Moore, Yeats spoke freely of his mystical views, noting that his basic symbols were sun and moon, mask and hawk, tower and tree. His work, he said, was "not drama but the ritual of a lost faith."

Independently, Joyce was pursuing the same dual aim: unity of vision amid progressively subtle modes of pre-sentation. His subject remained the ethos of Dublin, but successive treatments showed more profound insights, more complex associations. The philosophic perspective grew to cosmic (and comic) heights. His autobiographical manuscript *Stephen Hero* became intensified and univer-salized in the rewriting. The hero's life was no longer a mere succession of episodes, but a sequence of pivotal ex-periences: awareness of self, of family, of words, of sexual stimulation, of religious fear, of artistic awakening. The result is that *A Portrait of the Artist* remains one of the most intense and one of the most carefully articulated of novels.

His style was meanwhile becoming more virtuosic. The

everyday prose of *Stephen Hero* was succeeded by the evocative style of *Dubliners*. "Words alone are certain good," Yeats wrote in 1885. Ten years later the young Joyce was poring over Walter W. Skeat's *Etymological English Dictionary* (1879–82). Ever proud of his verbal skill, he used words precisely, even preciously, in his early stories. A young girl's figure is "defined" by a hall light (*Araby*); the fingers of a street harpist "careered" along the strings (*Two Gallants*). In the *Portrait*, style becomes substance; diction and syntax are adapted to the growing sensibility, from childhood simplicity to adolescent rapture. Like Yeats, Joyce sought precision and concreteness; constantly amplifying, he widened the range of implication. In outlook Yeats moved from romantic retreat, and Joyce from satiric rejection, to final acceptance of the real world.

In *Ulysses*, Joyce discovered the poetry of the actual. He often remarked to his friends that his imagination had never left Dublin, even though he spent his adult life in Trieste, Zurich, and Paris. The lanes and thoroughfares of his native city took on a patina of historical associations and personal memories. As a scrubby, unwashed youngster he had played in the alleyways of North Richmond Street; he had attended school under the Jesuits in the eighteenth-century mansion Belvedere House, whose elaborate plaster work on walls, staircases, and ceilings recalls the days when Dublin was a center of gracious living. Later he carried on his college studies at the Royal University in another mansion facing on St. Stephens Green, one of the most pleasant of European parks, lined on all sides by rows of handsome town houses. His mind was stored with literature—Latin, French, Italian, Elizabethan—and as he walked through the city, alone or with friends, his thoughts mingled ribaldry and poetry. These streets and stately public buildings would always be more than mere brick and stone to him. At times they would recall the grandeur of the classic age in which they were built; at times they would reflect the sordid poverty which his family shared with thousands of Dublin laborers. Love and hope and ambition and rebellion seethed in his heart.

In 1904, Joyce had left Dublin, a haughty exile. He then thought he could show his little world that his idol Ibsen had not died without a successor. But ten years brought him little enough, and Dubliners might well mock at the comeuppance Jimmy had had to take from life. With bad teeth and failing eyesight, his mind and temper were worn by his ill-paid teaching position in Trieste. In addition the difficulties of raising two children and supporting a wife were enough to excuse indefinite postponement of literary efforts. But the Dublin mockers—if any of them still thought of him at all—were wrong. Even though he had spent eight years wrangling with publishers, his volume of short stories, *Dubliners*, was about to appear in the summer of 1914. More important, his autobiographical novel, completely rewritten, was being printed in installments in the English *Egoist*. And even though he had written to his brother that "the chase of perfection is very unprofitable," he was beginning to find perfection within reach.

And there was, too, a new sense of responsibility. "Sometimes thinking of Ireland," he mused in another letter, "it seems to me that I have been unnecessarily harsh." The *Dubliners* stories, he continued, convey "none of the attraction of the city, for I have never felt at my ease in any city since I left it, except Paris." In particular, "its hospitality . . . so far as I can see, does not exist elsewhere in Europe," and "I have not been just to its beauty; for it is more beautiful naturally, in my opinion, than what I have seen of England, Switzerland, France, Austria and Italy."

The balance could be righted. He would describe Dublin so accurately that the city could be reconstructed from his novel. Had he not always played the game of naming streets and shops with his Dublin friends? But if his Baedeker was Thom's *Official Directory* of Dublin, it would take a convocation of commentators to trace his use of Biblical, Masonic, Catholic, Jewish, Irish, literary, musical, and philosophical lore. Joyce, as Harry Levin so wisely remarked, took all knowledge for his playground.

He would pursue a new purpose. The ageless saga of man the adventurer, the *Odyssey*, a schoolboy favorite—is it not repeated generation after generation, in city streets as well as on the high seas? Can Odysseus, called by Homer the man of many devices, be found in such a fumbling householder as he himself, the underpaid language teacher —or better, in his favorite pupil, the witty Jew Ettore Schmitz, manager of a paint company? And if Homer granted Odysseus the opportunity of escaping the Cyclops by means of a pun, would not *Ulysses* give rein to all Joyce's delight in verbal mockery? For Odysseus, it will be remembered, told the Cyclops that "Outis" (No Man) was his name, so that the wounded giant, blinded in his one eye, ran down the hillside screaming, "No man has hurt me." Joyce was at this time described by his pupil Schmitz as "a man who considers things as points breaking the light for his amusement."—The same composition noted his gentleness: "He is going through life hoping not to meet bad men. I wish him heartily not to meet them." On the

whole Joyce was luckier than most men in mid-Europe
from 1914 to 1939. The wishes of his Jewish friend tided
him well; he met few bad men. He escaped both wars, attained international fame, and, perhaps most important of
all, overcame his bitterness.

The Celtic Twilight lingered into the deepening shadows of the twentieth century, and it is appropriate that
night should at last fall in 1939, when nightmare rode the
imagination of man. In retrospect the flowering of Anglo-
Irish culture was to appear Arcadian, although in fact its
fifty-year history had seldom been free from strife and violence. The last major works of this movement are singu-
larly appropriate to the time. In the autumn of 1938, when
the world was trembling before the threats of Hitler, Yeats
had written his last great testament, the poem "Under Ben
Bulben." At the same time James Joyce, tormented by
family troubles and racked with self-doubt, was concluding his encylopedic, multilingual dream-book, *Finnegans
Wake*. Yeats died in January, 1939, just fifty years after the
publication of his first major volume of poetry, *The Wanderings of Oisin*. Joyce lived for two more unhappy years,
fleeing Paris at the time of Hitler's invasion, and, ever the
exile, finally escaping from unoccupied France to neutral
Switzerland just one month before his death.

"Under Ben Bulben" is a magnificent utterance, consoli-
dating the poet's position in the national ethos, and setting
the epigraph on a half-century of achievement. It recapitu-
lates the heroic themes of former works. The ancient sages
reappear, together with the legendary horsemen and the
mythic superhuman women. The aging poet faces death
with stoic faith in the continuity of the great cycles of
destiny. Strong though gravediggers be, they can only

"thrust their buried men/ Back in the human mind again." Death itself may be but one more form of that life-giving ecstasy of violence, that tragic joy in which all great deeds are achieved. Throughout the sweep of the historical process the task of the artist remains the same, to "bring the soul of man to God." In this task the Irish poet is especially privileged, heir to a unique destiny and spokes-man of a culture which for centuries has received the con-tributions of lord and laborer, saint and scholar. Thus, amid the vast concourses of history, two things remain steadfast: the spiritual goal of art and the tradition of the nation. And so, too, Yeats can return to his inheritance, his body in the churchyard of his grandfather's church at Drumcliff, the legend-haunted mass of Ben Bulben on the horizon, an ancient Irish cross near by, and on the stone an epitaph reminiscent of Swift's noble words, bidding the passer-by imitate the nobility of the dead hero.

Joyce finally, after seventeen years of meditation on his-tory, ransacking the world's cultures for pun or portent, was to project the same shadowy symbols as did Yeats, and to return, like Yeats, to humble filial piety. In a vision more pantheistic than that of Yeats, tree and stone, cloud and river remain as ever-changing witnesses to the eternal cycles of the generations of mankind. Both writers share the ancient belief that there is a uniquely Celtic insight, a quality evoked by Irish literature and legend. Although Irish in origin, this spirit is universal. He who could read its meaning might possess a sacred book and know the soul of man.

Chronology, 1885-1941

1885   Poems by William Butler Yeats first published in *Dublin University Review.*
Dublin Hermetic Society formed, Yeats presiding, June 16.

1886   Gladstone's first Home Rule Bill defeated in House of Commons.

1887   Yeats moves to London, and is active in theosophical groups.

1888 Anthology, *Poems and Ballads of Young Ireland,* edited by Yeats and others.

Patrick Weston Joyce, *Irish Music and Song.*

1889   Yeats meets Maud Gonne; publishes first book, *The Wanderings of Oisin.*

1890   Yeats, "The Lake Isle of Innisfree," *National Observer,* December.
Charles Stewart Parnell rejected as leader of Irish Parliamentary party.

1891   Yeats a founding member of Rhymers' Club, London, and of Irish Literary Society, London.
        Death of Parnell.

1892   Yeats a founding member of Irish National Literary Society, Dublin, opening programs of which were Dr. George Sigerson, "Irish Literature," August 16, and Douglas Hyde, "The Necessity for the De-Anglicising of the Irish Nation," November 25.
        Yeats, *The Countess Kathleen and Various Legends and Lyrics*.

1893   Yeats, *The Celtic Twilight*; Ellis-Yeats edition, *The Works of William Blake*; Yeats addresses Irish National Literary Society on "Nationality and Literature," May 19.
        Douglas Hyde, editor, *The Love Songs of Connacht*.
        Gaelic League formed.

1894   Yeats's play *The Land of Heart's Desire* at Avenue Theatre, London, March.
        Æ, *Homeward: Songs by the Way*.
        The Revival of Irish Literature (addresses by Sir Charles Gavan Duffy, Douglas Hyde, and Dr. George Sigerson).
        W. P. Ryan, *The Irish Literary Revival*.
        The New Ireland Review, edited by Rev. T. A. Finlay, March, 1894–February, 1911.

1895   Yeats, *Poems*, with many revisions; *A Book of Irish Verse*; articles on "Irish National Literature," *The Bookman*, July–October.
        "John Eglinton" (W. K. Magee), *Two Essays on the Remnant*.

1896 Yeats meets Lady Gregory during the summer, and John M. Synge in Paris, December.

William Sharp and J. Matthay, editors, *Lyra Celtica* (anthology).

1897 Yeats, *The Secret Rose*; *The Tables of the Law and The Adoration of the Magi.*

Sigerson, editor, *Bards of the Gael and Gall.*

First Feis Ceoil ("Music Festival"); Edward Martyn discusses project of Irish theatre with George Moore and Yeats.

Dublin riots in protest against Queen Victoria Jubilee.

1898 Synge makes first visit to Aran Islands.

Moore, *Evelyn Innes.*

T. P. Gill editor of Dublin *Daily Express*, July, 1898–December, 1899.

Theobald Wolfe Tone centennial commemoration, August 15.

1899 "Fiona MacLeod" (William Sharp), "A Group of Celtic Writers," *Fortnightly Review*, January.

Irish Literary Theatre: Yeats, *The Countess Cathleen*, May 8; Martyn, *The Heather Field*, May 9.

Yeats, *The Wind among the Reeds.*

Hyde, *A Literary History of Ireland.*

Literary Ideals in Ireland (essays by Æ, John Eglinton, William Larminie, and W. B. Yeats, from the Dublin *Daily Express*).

Irish Texts Society, Vol. I.

Exhibition of Sketches from the West of Ireland by Jack Butler Yeats.

The United Irishman, edited by Arthur Griffith, weekly, March 4, 1899–April 14, 1906. [Most influential voice for political change.]

An Claidheamh Soluis ("Sword of Light"), edited
by Eoin MacNeill and Padraic Pearse, 1899–1918.
[Organ of the Gaelic League.]

Beltaine ("May"), edited by W. B. Yeats, May, 1899,
February and April, 1900. [Irish Literary Theatre.]

In Africa, John MacBride forms Irish Brigade to aid
Boers against England.

1900   Joyce, in second year at the Royal University (now
University College), reads a paper, "Drama and
Life," at the Literary and Historical Society,
January 20, and publishes essay, "Ibsen's New
Drama," *Fortnightly Review*, April.

Queen Victoria visits Ireland; protests by Maud
Gonne, James Connolly, and others.

Irish Literary Theatre: Martyn, *Maeve,* and Alice
Milligan, *The Last Feast of the Fianna,* February 19; Moore, *The Bending of the Bough,* February 20.

Stopford A. Brooke and T. W. Rolleston, editors,
A Treasury of Irish Poetry.

All-Ireland Review, edited by Standish O'Grady,
January 6, 1900—April 31, 1906.

The Leader, edited by D. P. Moran, September 1,
1900–.

1901   Lady Gregory, editor, *Ideals in Ireland.*

Eglinton, *Pebbles from a Brook.*

Joyce, *The Day of the Rabblement,* in Joyce and
Francis Skeffington, *Two Essays.*

Moore, *Evelyn Innes* (second version).

Irish Literary Theatre: Yeats and Moore, *Diarmuid and Grania,* and Hyde, *Casadh an tSugain
("Twisting of the Rope"),* October 21.

Samhain ("All-Hallow Tide"), edited by W. B. Yeats, seven issues, 1901–1906 and 1908. [Theatre.]

1902   Joyce reads essay on Mangan, Literary and Historical Society, February 2; "James Clarence Mangan," in *St. Stephen's*, May.

Irish National Dramatic Company: Æ, *Deirdre*, and Yeats, *Cathleen ni Houlihan*, with Maud Gonne, April 2.

First American literary visitors: John Quinn, patron and collector, and Professor Cornelius Weygandt.

Joyce meets Æ and Yeats in summer, leaves Dublin in November for London and Paris, returning in April, 1903. Book reviews, Dublin *Daily Express*, December 11, 1902–November 19, 1903.

Lady Gregory, *Cuchulain of Muirthemne*.

Moore, *An t-Úr Ghort ("The Untilled Field")*, a translation into Irish by Pádraig Ó Súilleabáin.

Stephen Gwynn, *To-Day and To-Morrow in Ireland*.

1903   Irish National Theatre Society visits London, May 2; premiere of Synge on October 8, *In the Shadow of the Glen*.

James Gordon Bennett automobile race (see Joyce, *After the Race*); Edward VII visits Ireland (see Joyce, *Ivy Day in the Committee Room*).

Yeats goes to America on speaking tour (October, 1903–March, 1904); *In the Seven Woods*, first publication of Dun Emer, later Cuala, Press; *Ideas of Good and Evil* (essays on symbolism).

Moore, *The Untilled Field*.

Wyndham Land Purchase Act alleviates farm conditions; landowners' conference suggested by Captain John Shawe-Taylor, nephew of Lady Gregory.

1904   Joyce essay, "A Portrait of the Artist," rejected by *Dana*, first published, *Yale Review*, Spring, 1960; wins medal in singing contest, May 16; teaches in Dalkey, meets Nora Barnacle; sings in concert, August 27, John McCormack on program (see Joyce, *A Mother*); leaves Dublin with Nora.

Date of action in Joyce's *Ulysses*, June 16.

Joyce, *The Holy Office*, broadside, October; three stories in *Irish Homestead*, August–December; poem in *Dana*, August.

Rev. Peter O'Leary, *Séadna*, in Irish.

Hyde, *An Cleamhnas ("The Matchmaking")*, in Irish.

Rev. P. S. Dineen, *Foclóir Gaedhilge and Béarla* (Irish dictionary).

Irish National Theatre Society: Synge, *Riders to the Sea*, February 25; opening of Abbey Theatre, December 27, with Lady Gregory, *Spreading the News*, and Yeats, *On Baile's Strand*.

Æ, editor, *New Songs* (anthology of younger poets).

Dana, edited by John Eglinton and Frederick Ryan, May, 1904–April, 1905.

Moore, *The Lake*.

Arthur Griffith, *The Resurrection of Hungary*.

Exhibit of paintings by Æ and Constance Gore-Booth Markiewicz, September.

Exhibit of paintings from Staat-Forbes collection, November, which Hugh Lane suggests making core of Dublin gallery.

1905   Joyce in Trieste, March; joined by brother Stanislaus, October.

Abbey Theatre reorganization leads to resignation of many actors.

Griffith outlines Hungarian policy of separate parliament at first National Sinn Fein Convention.

The Nationist, edited by Thomas Kettle, weekly, September 21, 1905–April 5, 1906. [Parliamentary liberalism of Young Ireland branch.]

1906   Theatre of Ireland formed, May, with Edward Martyn president, and Padraic Colum, Padraic Pearse, and Thomas Kettle on committee. Programs: December, 1906; two annually, 1907–10; three annually, 1911–12.

Joyce in Rome, July, 1906–March, 1907.

The Arrow, edited by W. B. Yeats, five issues, 1906–1909. [Abbey Theatre.]

The Shanachie, edited by Joseph Hone, six issues, 1906–1907.

Sinn Fein, edited by Arthur Griffith, May 5, 1906–November 28, 1914.

1907   Abbey Theatre: rioting at Synge's *The Playboy of the Western World,* January.

Joyce, *Chamber Music.*

Synge, *The Aran Islands,* illustrated by Jack Butler Yeats.

Rev. Peter O'Leary, *Niamh,* in Irish.

Padraic Pearse, *Iosagán agus Sgealta eile ("Little Jesus and Other Stories").*

Yeats travels in Italy with Lady Gregory and her son Robert.

1908   Yeats, *Collected Works,* eight volumes.

Opening of Municipal Gallery of Art.

Abbey Theatre: resignation of Willie and Frank Fay.

1909   Abbey Theatre: Synge dies, March 24; Dunsany premiere, *The Glittering Gate*, April 29; production of Shaw's *The Showing up of Blanco Posnet*, August 25, in defiance of censorship in London.

Theatre of Ireland: Seumas O'Kelly's *The Shuiler's Child*, April 29, with Countess Markievicz and James Stephens in cast.

Joyce in Dublin twice, August, and October 21–January, 1910.

Yeats meets Ezra Pound.

Pearse founds Irish school for boys, St. Enda's.

Gregory, *Seven Short Plays*.

Moore, *Evelyn Innes* (third version).

1910   Yeats, *The Green Helmet and Other Poems*.

Kettle, *The Day's Burden*.

1911   Abbey Theatre: first American tour, September–March, protests in Boston, New York, and Philadelphia. Tours in 1912–13 and 1913–14.

Moore leaves Ireland. First volume, *Ave*, of *Hail and Farewell*.

The Irish Review, edited by Joseph Mary Plunkett, forty-four issues, 1911–14.

1912   James Stephens, *The Crock of Gold* and *The Charwoman's Daughter*.

Joyce's last visit to Dublin, July–September; *Gas from a Burner*.

Beginnings of military organization in Ulster to protest against Home Rule for Ireland, Ulster Volunteers.

Moore, second volume, *Salve*, of *Hail and Farewell*.

1913   First important studies of Irish literary revival:
       Lady Gregory, *Our Irish Theatre*; Cornelius Wey-
       gandt, *Irish Plays and Playwrights*; Katherine
       Tynan Hinkson, *Twenty-five Years*.
       Dublin lockout (August, 1913–February, 1914);
       Irish Citizen Army (Labor) formed, October;
       Irish Volunteers, November; England prohibits
       arms importation.
       Dublin Corporation rejects Hugh Lane's proposed
       art gallery.

1914   Joyce, *Dubliners*; begins writing *Ulysses*.
       Yeats, *Responsibilities*; American lecture tour.
       Moore, final volume, *Vale*, of *Hail and Farewell*.
       Pearse, *Suantraidhe agus Goltraidhe ("Lullaby and
       Lament")*.
       Irish Theatre, under direction of Edward Martyn,
       Thomas MacDonagh, and Joseph Mary Plunkett,
       November 2. Six programs in 1915, one in 1916.
       Irish Volunteer, edited by Laurence de Lacey and
       Eoin MacNeill, 1914–16.
       Curragh "Mutiny," refusal of troops to hinder raids
       for arms by Ulster Volunteers, March 20; arms
       landed at Larne for Ulster with no opposition,
       April 24, but Howth landing, July 26, results in
       troops' firing on Dublin crowd. Estimated 85,000
       in Ulster Volunteers, 132,000 in Irish. Declara-
       tion of war postpones application of Home Rule,
       splits Irish Volunteers, the extreme national-
       ists, 10,000, electing Professor Eoin MacNeill
       head, October. Secret council of Irish Republi-
       can Brotherhood plans rising. Insurgent periodi-
       cals suppressed, December.

1915   Yeats, *Reveries*; makes long visits to Ezra Pound in

England, spring and winter. Studies of his work by Forrest Reid and J. M. Hone.

Abbey Theatre: St. John Ervine, *John Ferguson,* November 30.

Joyce comes to Zurich to live for duration of the war.

Hugh Lane drowned on *Lusitania,* starting controversy over unwitnessed codicil bequeathing pictures to Dublin.

New Ireland, edited by Denis Gwynn and P. J. Little, 1915–19.

Parades and maneuvers in Dublin; Pearse speaks at huge demonstration for funeral of Jeremiah O'Donovan Rossa, August 1.

1916   Joyce, *A Portrait of the Artist as a Young Man.*
Moore, *The Brook Kerith.*

Lennox Robinson, *The Whiteheaded Boy,* December 13.

Ernest A. Boyd, *Ireland's Literary Renaissance;* Darrell Figgis, *A.E.;* Thomas MacDonagh, *Literature in Ireland.*

Yeats produces his first play for dancers, *At the Hawk's Well,* London.

Easter Rising, April 24–30. Fifteen executed, May 3–12; deportation of 1,700 to English prisons; trial and execution of Roger Casement, August; release of prisoners, December.

1917   Yeats marries George Hyde-Lees; *The Wild Swans at Coole;* buys tower, County Galway.

Sinn Fein wins Parliamentary seats—Count Plunkett, February 5; Joseph McGuinness (by 37-vote margin), May 9; Eamon de Valera, July 11; W. T. Cosgrave, August 10. Deportations, February

26; releases, June 16; further arrests, August 15. Burial of Thomas Ashe, victim of mistreatment in prison, September 30.

Sinn Fein Convention, October 25–27, replaces Griffith with de Valera and adopts more Republican stand. De Valera is elected head of Volunteers, making him leader of both Republican organizations.

Lloyd George calls Irish Convention (conference on Home Rule), July 25, 1917–April 5, 1918.

1918   Joyce, *Exiles*; *Ulysses* begins to appear in *Little Review*, March.

Parliament votes conscription for Ireland, April 18; widespread protests; suppression of meetings and arrest of de Valera, Maud Gonne MacBride, Griffith, and others for presumed "German plot," May 17.

General election, December 14, makes sweep of Sinn Fein candidates in Southern Ireland, 69 members, 34 of whom are in prison.

1919   Seumas O'Kelly, *The Golden Barque and The Weaver's Grave*.

Padraic O'Conaire, *An Crann Géagach ("The Branching Tree")*.

First Dail meets in Dublin, January 21, declares independence, elects de Valera president, Cathal Brugha acting president. Raid on Royal Irish Constabulary opens war. De Valera escapes from prison, February 3, goes to United States (June, 1919–December, 1920). Dail proclaimed dangerous and newspapers suppressed, September; terrorism increases; attempted assassination of Lord French, lord lieutenant of Ireland, December 19.

The Republic, edited by Darrell Figgis, June 21–
September 20.

The Irish Bulletin, edited by Frank Gallagher, Desmond Fitzgerald, and Erskine Childers, November 11, 1919–December 13, 1921.

1920   Yeats on American tour.

Joyce moves to Paris, June.

Increasing violence with arrival of "Black and
Tans," March; hunger strike, Mountjoy Prison,
Dublin, April; Terence MacSwiney, lord mayor
of Cork, becomes a national hero, dying in Brix-
ton Jail, London, October 25, after seventy-four-
day hunger strike. Collins directs counterespionage. "Bloody Sunday," November 21, fourteen
English Army suspects killed in lodgings, Dublin; in afternoon, auxiliaries fire into a Dublin
football crowd, Croke Park. Griffith and Mac-
Neill arrested, November 26. Cork burned, December 11, damage of £3,000,000.

English Parliament passes Government of Ireland
Act, providing for two Irish parliaments, one to
meet in Belfast (six counties), the other in Dublin (twenty-six counties).

1921   Moore, *Heloise and Abelard*.

Elections for parliaments called for in Government
of Ireland Act, May 24. Only in Northern Ireland are Sinn Fein candidates opposed, where
they win six seats. Meeting in Dublin, August,
Sinn Fein members consider themselves a Second
Dail, not a Southern Ireland Parliament. Meanwhile, only four members and fifteen senators attend Parliament of Southern Ireland, June 28,
and disband.

English records destroyed in firing of Dublin Customs House, May 25.

Truce, effective July 11. Delegates confer in London on Treaty.

Treaty signed in London, December 6: dominion status and partition. Treaty debates split Dail.

1922 Joyce, *Ulysses*, published in Paris, February.

Yeats in Free State Senate, 1922–28.

Treaty ratified, 64–57, January 9; de Valera resigns presidency, loses re-election, 58–60. Southern Ireland has four "governments": Dail (Griffith, president), the allied Provisional government under Michael Collins, the disaffected Republicans under de Valera, and the army under Rory O'Connor. O'Connor's troops seize Four Courts as headquarters, April 13.

In an attempt to avoid armed conflict, Collins and de Valera make a pact on May 20, agreeing to a coalition slate in the forthcoming election, to be held under legislation consequent on the Treaty. Coalition of 68 Treaty and 58 Republican members would maintain *status quo*. Pact renounced by Provisional government, June 14, and constitution publicized on morning of election, June 16. Results: 58 Treaty, 35 Republican.

Field Marshal Sir Henry Wilson assassinated in London, June 22; ultimatum given to Republican Army; Four Courts attacked, June 28–30, and Republicans defeated in Dublin, July, after which guerrilla combat continues.

Poblacht na h-Eireann ("Republic of Ireland"), edited by Erskine Childers [anti-Treaty], January 3–June 29, 1922, after which *War News*, to March 16, 1923.

Arthur Griffith dies, August 12, and Michael Collins is killed, August 22.

Third Dail (first of Provisional government) meets, September 9, gives emergency powers, under which Erskine Childers is executed, November 24. Campaign of terror against government leaders, with assassinations and house-burnings. In reprisal, O'Connor and three other Republicans are executed, December 8.

Free State established, December 6.

1923   Yeats is awarded Nobel Prize.

O'Casey, *The Shadow of a Gunman*, April 9.

Gogarty, *An Offering of Swans.*

The Dublin Magazine, edited by Seumas O'Sullivan, August 1923–October, 1957.

The Irish Statesman, edited by Æ, September 15, 1923–August 12, 1930.

Final outburst of violence by I.R.A. Cease-fire, May. De Valera confined for year without trial, August 15, 1923–July 16, 1924.

1924   O'Casey, *Juno and the Paycock*, March 3.

1925   Yeats, *A Vision.*

Liam O'Flaherty, *The Informer.*

Daniel Corkery, *The Hidden Ireland.*

1926   O'Casey, *The Plough and the Stars*, February 8.

1927   Abbey Theatre rejects O'Casey's *The Silver Tassie.*

Kevin O'Higgins assassinated, July 10; de Valera leads followers into Dail.

1928   Joyce, *Anna Livia Plurabelle.*

Yeats, *The Tower.*

Rev. Richard Henebry, *A Handbook of Irish Music.*
Gate Theatre opens.

1929 Gate Theatre: Denis Johnston, *The Old Lady Says "No."*
Corkery, *The Stormy Hills.*

1930 Stuart Gilbert, *James Joyce's "Ulysses."*

1931 Abbey Theatre: Johnston, *The Moon in the Yellow River.*

1932 Frank O'Connor, *The Saint and Mary Kate.*
De Valera wins control of Dail, March.
Irish Academy.

1933 Yeats, *The Winding Stair and Other Poems.*
Maurice O'Sullivan, *Fiche Blian ag Fás ("Twenty Years A-Growing").*
Sean O'Faolain, *A Nest of Simple Folk.*

1934 Joyce, *Ulysses* (first printing in English-speaking world), New York.

1935 Frank Pakenham, *Peace by Ordeal.*
Eglinton, *Irish Literary Portraits.*

1936 Yeats, *Dramatis Personae.*
Ernie O'Malley, *On Another Man's Wound.*

1937 O'Flaherty, *Famine.*
Gogarty, *As I was Going down Sackville Street.*
Abbey Theatre: Paul Vincent Carroll, *Shadow and Substance*, January 25.

1938 Abbey Theatre Festival; Yeats makes last public appearance, a curtain call after his *Purgatory.*
Samuel Beckett, *Murphy.*

1939   Yeats dies, January 28.

Joyce, *Finnegans Wake*; leaves Paris, December, for southern France.

Flann O'Brian, *At Swim-Two-Birds*.

O'Casey, *I Knock at the Door* (first volume of seven-volume autobiography, *Mirror in My House*, 1939–45).

1940   Joyce reaches Zurich, December.

1941   Joyce dies, January 13.

Selected Bibliography

THE LITERARY REVIVAL:

The best guide to the literary revival, even though it is much out of date—with Joyce scarcely known, and Yeats having his best years ahead—is Ernest A. Boyd's *Ireland's Literary Renaissance* (Dublin, 1916; N.Y., 1922). "John Eglinton's" (W. K. Magee's) *Irish Literary Portraits* (London, 1935) is a series of perceptive accounts of Yeats, Æ, Moore, and Joyce, by one who knew them all. Herbert Howarth, in *The Irish Writers, 1880–1940: Literature under Parnell's Star* (London, 1958), gives unusual appraisals of political and psychological factors of the revival. A fine pioneer study of the movement is Cornelius Weygandt's *Irish Plays and Playwrights* (N. Y., 1913). There are also surveys of modern Anglo-Irish literature by Stephen Gwynn (1936), Hugh Law (1926), Thomas MacDonagh (1916), Lloyd Morris (1917), and W. P. Ryan (1894). On the Abbey Theatre one may refer to the books by Ernest Boyd (1917), Dawson Byrne (1929), Gerard

Fay (1958), W. G. Fay and C. Carswell (1935), Una Ellis-Fermor (1939), Lady Gregory (1913), Peter Kavanagh (1950), Brinsley Macnamara (1949), Lennox Robinson, *et al.* (1939), and Lennox Robinson (1951). Fine anthologies of modern Irish poetry in English are by William Butler Yeats (1895), Stopford A. Brooke and T. W. Rolleston (1900), Lennox Robinson (1925), and Donagh MacDonagh and Lennox Robinson (1958). Recent short-story anthologies have been compiled by Frank O'Connor (1957), Devin A. Garrity (1957, 1960), and Valentin Iremonger (1960).

REMINISCENCES:

As I Was Going down Sackville Street, by Oliver St. John Gogarty (N. Y., 1937), is the first and best of his many delightful volumes. Its subtitle, "A Phantasy in Fact," should warn but not deter readers. The classic of Irish fantasy-and-fact is George Moore's *Hail and Farewell* (London, 1911–14). William Butler Yeats's *Autobiographies* (London, 1914–35) are poetic impressions, always rewarding. Other fascinating books of reminiscences are: Lady Gregory (edited by Lennox Robinson), *Journals* (N. Y., 1946); Katherine Tynan Hinkson, *Twenty-five Years* (London, 1913); and Sean O'Casey, *The Mirror in the House* (N. Y., 1939–54). One may also consult the memoirs of Mary Butler, J. F. Byrne (the "Cranly" of Joyce's fiction), Mary Colum, James and Margaret Cousins, Page Dickinson, St. John G. Ervine, Stephen Gwynn, Stanislaus Joyce, Maud Gonne MacBride, Stephen MacKenna, Lennox Robinson, Maire Nic Shiubhlaigh ("Mary Walker"), Seumas O'Sullivan, Eugene Sheehy, Terence de Vere White, and many recollections by political leaders.

Selected Bibliography

POLITICAL HISTORY:

The Irish Republic, by Dorothy MacArdle (London, 1937), is detailed and anti-Treaty. The outstanding literary achievement of the Anglo-Irish war, by a field officer, Ernie O'Malley, is *On Another Man's Wound* (Dublin, 1936). An American edition the following year, *Army without Banners*, contains passages omitted from the original edition. Donal O'Sullivan gives an intelligent and scholarly defense of the Treaty, and a history of the early years of the Free State and its upper house, in *The Irish Free State and Its Senate* (London, 1940). Frank Pakenham's *Peace by Ordeal* (London, 1935) examines the 1921 Treaty. The most complete history of Easter week, 1916, is by Desmond Ryan, *The Rising* (Dublin, 1957); while *The Insurrection in Dublin*, by James Stephens (London, 1916), is the best contemporary account.

GENERAL:

A civic, cultural, and architectural history of value is John Harvey's *Dublin: A Study of Environment* (London, 1949). Other good general books on Ireland and its people are Sean O'Faolain's *The Irish* (London, 1947) and Arland Ussher's *The Face and Mind of Ireland* (London, 1950).

Index

Index

Index